COVER

The sign shown on the cover is a combination of the letters "I," "L" and "Y." Originally deaf school children used it among themselves to mean, "I love you." In recent years, however, the sign has gained wide popularity and has become almost a gesture-symbol, much like the "V" that young hearing people often used for "peace" a few years ago or like the "thumbs up" sign associated with the unsinkable British during World War II. The "I-L-Y" sign may still mean, "I love you," but it may also be a sign of welcome, of greeting, of a way to say, "I'm for sign language!" and a host of other meanings.

FOURTH-MOST-USED-LANGUAGE

The claim that American Sign Language (AMESLAN or A.S.L.) is the "fourth-most-used" language in the United States is based on the September, 1974, issue of "ASHA" (Journal of the American Speech and Hearing Association). According to that publication Sign Language ranks third as a foreign language in the United States, with just under 500,000 deaf persons using Sign Language to communicate. Spanish is number one with 4.5 million users and Italian is second with 631,000. The findings were revealed in research conducted in connection with proposed federal legislation to include deaf persons in the Bilingual Courts Act. Following Sign Language are French, 414,000; German, 251,000; and Yiddish, 26,000.

SIGN LANGUAGE

by
LOU FANT

© JOYCE MEDIA, INC. 1977

First Printing . . . . December 1977
Second Printing. . . . . April 1978
Third Printing. . . . . October 1978
Fourth Printing. . . . . .March 1979
Fifth Printing . . . . .July 1979
Sixth Printing. . . . . .February 1980

ISBN—0-917002-13-x
Library of Congress Number—77-93544

Photographed and Designed by John Joyce
Cover Drawings by Stephanie Pyren
Written by Lou Fant

Printed in the United States of America

For information concerning this publication please contact:

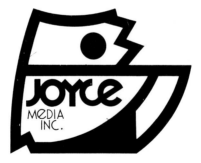

JOYCE MEDIA, INC.
8753 Shirley
PO Box 458
Northridge, California 91328

Telephone (213) 885-7181 (Voice or TTY)

DEDICATED TO

Ameslan
which
molds space into meanings
that
touch the mind and heart

ACKNOWLEDGEMENT

I wish to express my gratitude to Marina McIntire for her valuable assistance in preparing this book.

American Sign Language is also called AMESLAN or A.S.L..

INTRODUCTION

The study of Ameslan can be a fascinating and rewarding adventure, or it can be confusing and frustrating drudgery. Much depends upon one's attitude as one approaches the subject. Those who expect Ameslan to be a manual form of English are rudely shocked to find that it has as much in common with Chinese as English. Those who have heard that you have to be born to deaf parents in order to be fluent in Ameslan become anxious about their ability to learn the language.

Such misconceptions ought to be put away immediately. If you are of average intelligence, and you are motivated, you will learn Ameslan. There is no mystery about Ameslan, it yields itself to whomever desires to know it.

One thing only is required of you, and that is that you approach the study of Ameslan as you would approach the study of any language. Rid youself of preconceived notions as to the nature of Ameslan.

Imagine one's progress in Spanish if one continually complains about how silly it is to put adjectives after the words they modify. That type person asks, "Why do they do it that way? Why can't they do it the way we do?" It is linguistic chauvinism to think that all languages are inferior to English. Never ask "why" about a language, only "how".

If it is any solace to the reader, there are thousands of children of deaf parents who are totally inept in Ameslan. Merely having deaf parents does not insure fluency in Ameslan. There are also thousands of sons and daughters of immigrants who cannot speak the native language of their parents. Some of the best students I have had, came into my class never having met a deaf person.

The uniqueness of Ameslan lies in the simple fact that it is based upon light waves rather than sound waves. It is a visual, as opposed to an aural language. Meaning is conveyed by sight, not sound. So, the "listener" shall be referred to as the watcher, abbreviated: W, and the "speaker" shall be called the signer, abbreviated: S .

When S signs, W watches not just the hands, but also the whole of S: the speed and vigor of the signing, the size of the sign, the place a sign is made, the direction a sign moves, the facial expression, the head movements, the shoulder movements, the shape of the mouth and cheeks, the movement of the tongue, the movement and focus of the eyes, and the emotion of S. You communicate with your total being, not merely with your hands. You must commit yourself totally to the language.

There have been efforts to create symbols which make it possible to write signs. The difficulty with these symbols is that a separate course in writing Ameslan would be required in order to master it. Most students do not have the time this would require. Furthermore, deaf people write in English, so there would be little need for such mastery. However, in studying the language, we do need some convenient way to write it.

Strictly speaking, the only way to write Ameslan is to use motion pictures. Since that is not practical here, we use instead still photographs or drawings. However, we are still left with the difficulty of talking about the signs. In other words, what do we call the signs? The answer is that we give the signs English names.

This seems to be a suitably simple solution, but unfortunately it conceals a pitfall. The student too often thinks that the name of a sign is the meaning of the sign. A sign may have many meanings, just as words often have many meanings. The word, "run", for example has quite a few meanings:

> It's starting to rain, run for the office.
> He will run for office next year.
> She has a run in her stockings.
> They scored a run in the bottom of the third.
> How many copies did you run off?
> Have you heard, there's a run on cabbages this week?
> You're going to run into debt.
> My clock won't run.

just to mention a few. Let there be no complaints then about signs having more than one meaning!

The problem here is that the sign, RUN, means only to move in a hurry, as in the first example sentence above. The RUN sign cannot be used in any of the other sentences. The word "run" is used as a name, a label for the sign. So do not fall into the trap of thinking that the English word used to designate a sign, is the meaning of that sign. Each time a sign is introduced in this book you will be given the most common meanings of that sign, and you will be told the most common name for it.

In this book, the names of signs are always written in capitals: GIRL, COW, SCHOOL. Sometimes a name will consist of two or three words: GO-TO, UP-TILL-NOW. In such cases the words are hyphenated to indicate only one sign is intended. The single sign GO-TO is quite different from the two signs GO, TO. In writing the names of signs for your own notes use underlining. Fingerspelling is also written in capitals, but each letter is separated by dashes: G–I–R–L.

Ameslan consists of signs and fingerspelling. This book concentrates on signs, with only minimal attention given to fingerspelling. The reasons for this are:

1. Fingerspelling is based on the English alphabet. Thus, fingerspelling produces English words. If the student concentrates on fingerspelling, he will persist in thinking in English rather than Ameslan, thus his mastery of Ameslan will be impeded.
2. In ordinary, informal conversation among deaf people, fingerspelling constitutes less than 15% of the conversation.
3. Mastery of fingerspelling, particularly the reading of it, is difficult. A tremendous amount of time and energy must be invested in the acquisition of fluency in fingerspelling. Such investment leaves insufficient time to learn Ameslan. It is recommended that fingerspelling constitute a course in itself.

And now, if your mind has been sufficiently cleared of all prejudiced notions about Ameslan, and you believe you can learn Ameslan even though you have never clapped eyes on a deaf person, you are ready for the first lesson.

Lou Fant
Northridge
December 1977

PICTURE READING.

1.   The photographs in SIGN LANGUAGE will help you to learn how to form the signs. Read these pictures carefully so that you grasp the correct motions of the signs.

2. READ EACH PHOTOGRAPH FROM TOP TO BOTTOM AND FROM THE WATCHER'S LEFT TO RIGHT UNLESS DIRECTED TO DO OTHERWISE BY ONE OF THE ARROWS LISTED BELOW.

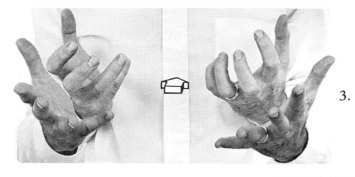

3.   Sign moves in toward the signer.

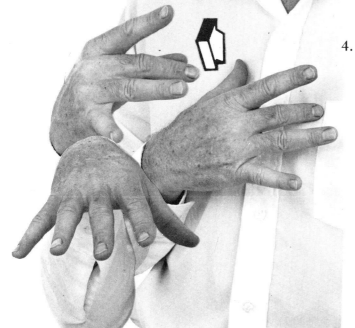

4.   Sign moves out from the signer toward the watcher.

5. Sign moves from the signer's right out past the watcher's left.

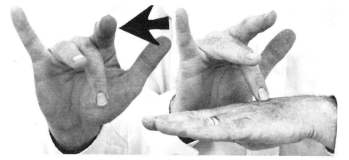

6. Sign moves in a flat plane from signer's left to right.

7. Sign moves from bottom to top.

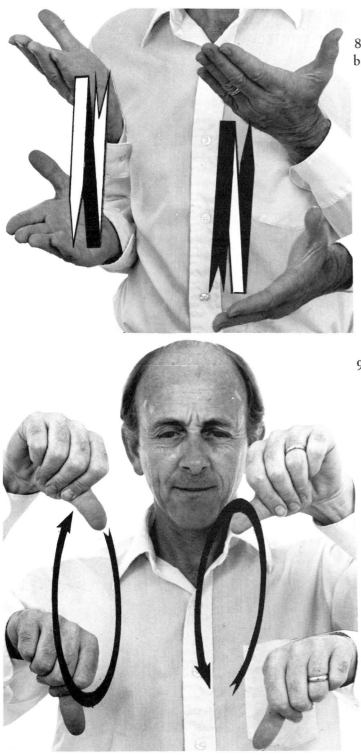

8. Hands alternate motions and go up and down or back and forth.

9. Hands alternate motions and go around in circles.

11. Repeat the same motion of the sign several times.

SIGNLINES

The following "Signlines" are an overview of things that are touched upon in this book. Use them just to get an idea of what you will be studying and come back to them from time to time for review.

All signs contain four basic components: (1) the shape of the hands, (2) the placement of the hands, that is, where the hands are at the beginning and ending of a sign, (3) the movement of the hands, and (4) the orientation of the hands, that is, how they are positioned with relation to the body and to each other.

Of these four components, movement is perhaps the most prominent. Even with inaccurately made signs, the movement alone will usually convey the meaning. This is evidenced by deaf people with malformed hands, or hands with fingers missing whose signing is still quite legible. Therefore, the beginning student should devote much attention to the movements of signs.

1. Signs in which the movement usually plays very little role other than being necessary to the execution of the sign: AND, HOME, COFFEE.

2. Movement which implies subject-object relationships: GIVE, HELP, ADVISE.

3. Movement alters the basic meaning of the sign: NICE vs. CLEAN, ALMOST vs. EASY, ONLY vs. ALWAYS.

4. Movement which implies quantities.

    A. Size

    (1) LARGE: by expanding the hands, one gets "huge," "collosal," etc.

    (2) CLOUD: by expanding the hands, one gets "an enormous cloud," or by contraction, one gets "a tiny cloud."

    B. Plurality–repetition of HOUSE gives "city;" repetition of TREE gives "forest."

    C. Shape is usually described by moving the hands or fingers to correspond with the shape of the object.

    (1) Geometric figures are outlined with the index fingers.

    (2) Containers are outlined with the hands.

    (3) A statue or loving cup is outlined with the thumbs.

    D. Weight

    (1) The sign HEAVY is varied to show how heavy an object is.

    (2) The sign VEHICLE may be varied to show its weight.

    (3) The signs RAIN and SNOW may be varied to show heavy or light rain and snow.

    E. Distance

    The INDEX sign shows greater distances when it is arced, or jiggled.

    (2) FAR is modified by arcing and tension.

    (3) The distance traveled by an airplane may be greatly increased by moving the AIRPLANE sign slowly and at the same time trembling the hand slightly.

    F. Area

    (1) The AREA sign is done larger or smaller to indicate the size of the area, which may vary from a tiny piece of land, to a whole continent.

    (2) TRAVEL may show how much area was covered in a trip.

5. Movement which implies physical relationships.

    A. MEET may be modified in numerous ways to show who meets whom, or in what relationship people physically stand to each other, i.e., facing each other, backs toward each other, etc.

B. FOLLOW may show how closely one follows, or at what rate one falls behind.

C. LOOK may show the action of people's eyes in observing each other.

6. Movement which implies some temporal element.

A. Duration--A sign may be done quickly or slowly to show the amount of time consumed. (EAT)

B. Speed--A sign may be done quickly or slowly to imply how quickly or slowly an event occurred. (WORK, READ)

C. Regularity--Repetition of a sign may imply the regularity with which the event occurs. (SICK, GO TO R/L)

D. Reiteration--Repetition of a sign may imply that an activity or event is done over and over again. (SAME, AGAIN, TALK)

7. Movement which implies subjective qualities.

A. Degrees of emotional affect may be shown by the movement. (LIKE, PLEASE, WANT, HATE, ANGRY)

B. Difficulty vs. ease may be shown by tensed vs. relaxed movement. (WORK, PLAY)

C. Degree of certainty may be shown by the vigor of the movement. (KNOW, TELL, SEE)

D. Adjectives may be intensified by more vigorous movement. (FINE, LOUSY)

8. Pantomime is frequently used: pouring, drinking, performance of a task, etc.

Naturally the facial expressions that accompany all signs are a necessary complement to the full meaning of the signs.

A Summary of Grammatical Points

1. Objects and persons are usually established with the appropriate sign for the object or person, followed by indexing.

2. Head tilts are incorporated in question forms.

3. Non-directional verb signs require signs for both subject and object.

4. Uni-directional verb signs require signs for subject and first person object; second and third person objects require no signs.

5. Multi-directional verb signs require no signs for subject or object.

6. Signs are frequently repeated or copied.

7. Persons and objects are frequently spatialized for ease of reference during conversation, and to create a clearer picture.

8. Sign order may be determined by putting more concrete objects before less concrete ones, e.g., noun before adjective.

9. Sign order may be determined by following the time sequence principle; events are reported in the chronological order in which they occurred.

10. Sign order may be determined by ease with which one sign blends into another; BOOK READ (holding LH in BOOK, while RH signs READ) is easier and clearer than READ BOOK.

11. Specific time-indicators usually come at the beginning of a sentence.

12. When FINISH is used as a time-indicator, it usually follows the verb sign.

13. Negatives usually follow the sign they negate.

14. Interrogatives come at the end of the question.

15. The FINISH sign may also be used to indicate that when one event was completed, another followed in sequence: "After we

ate, we left," "When we had eaten, we left," "We ate, then we left."

16. Sentences of three signs or less may usually be signed in any order.

17. The signs HAVE and TRUE sometimes mean "there is," "there are," "there was," "there were," etc.

18. Adjectives may be intensified by use of the COMPARATIVE MARKER, or by modifying the adjective sign.

19. Following the time-sequence principle, sign order may represent cause and effect, stimulus-response relationships, thus emotional responses follow that which causes or stimulates the responses.

20. In imperative statements, the operative sign comes last: GO NOW!, EAT MUST!.

21. The body shift is often used to report dialogue between two or more people.

22. The rhetorical question is frequently used in Ameslan: ME LIVE WHERE//HOUSE THAT-R INDEX-R//.

23. Whenever possible, show what is meant rather than tell what is meant, i.e., what you see is what you get.

NOTES

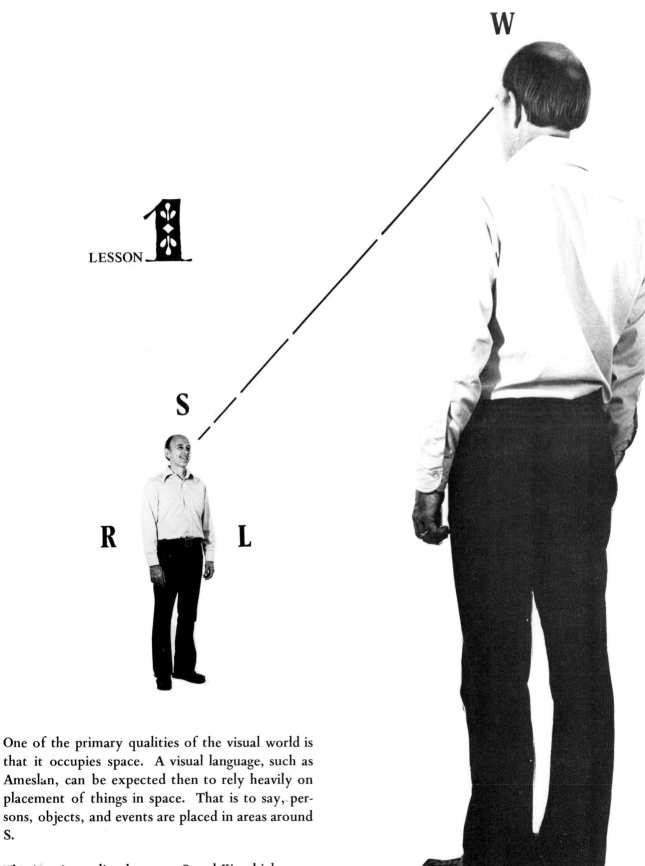

W

S

R **L**

One of the primary qualities of the visual world is that it occupies space. A visual language, such as Ameslan, can be expected then to rely heavily on placement of things in space. That is to say, persons, objects, and events are placed in areas around S.

The imaginary line between S and W, which separates the areas L (left) and R (right), is called the sight line (SL). The symbols L and R always refer to the areas to the left and right of S.

Pointing to W means "you" and is called YOU. Pointing to yourself means "me" or "I" and is called ME. If you point R or L, it means that S is referring to whatever has been established previously in those areas.

S

R

L

W

If, for example, S is telling W about meeting a friend, S will make the sign for friend in the R area. From then on, until something else is placed in R, each time S points to R, it may mean, "my friend," or "he/she".

R

W

If S places a book in R, then pointing R may mean, "the book," or "it."

If S places his bedroom in R, then pointing R may mean, "the bedroom," or "there."

In short, pointing R or L by itself has no meaning. Something must first be placed, established, or spatialized there before the pointing is meaningful.

Pointing L or R is called the IT sign, but the direction must always be written: IT-R or IT-L. Usually, IT-R is done with the right hand, and IT-L is done with the left hand.

IT-R

R   S   L

W

EXERCISE 1

Use both hands in various combinations.

you and I	she and he	him and me
you and it	he and it	you and she
he and I	her and it	she and it

IT-L

4

LESSON

In spoken English, the rise and fall of the voice adds clarity of meaning to a statement, and changes the meanings of the words. Think of all the ways you can say, "I love you." The words are always the same, but changes occur in the voice which alter the meaning. Just so, the face and head movement alter the meaning of signs, along with all those things mentioned in the introduction.

Sign YOU, and at the same time nod your head. This may mean, " Yes, you!" Sign, YOU and at the same time shake your head, "no." This may mean, "No, not you."

Exercise 2

Using only the three signs you have learned, convey as many meanings of each sentence as you can. Think the sentence to yourself as you make the signs, and make the appropriate facial expressions and head movements.

1. Yes, I do! (As if someone has just accused you of not doing something. You should point to yourself, nod your head, making the appropriate facial expression. Got it? Now try the same sentence, but with the attitude that you are answering someone's skeptical question, "You don't really do that, do you?")

2. Not you, dummy, him! (Sign YOU, shaking your head, "no," then sign IT-R shaking your head, "yes." Your facial expression might be one of exasperation, or of humor.....try both.)

3. It's he and she. (Sign IT-R with the right hand from now on abbreviated, RH--- and IT-L with the left hand---LH---and nod, "yes." You should be able to express several emotional attitudes with this sentence, e.g. strong affirmation, accusation, sly inference, etc.)

Use your imagination. Picture the persons you are talking about. Picture the scene in which you see those persons. Get your feeling about those persons in that scene clearly in mind, and show your feeling by facial expression and head movement.

4. No, it isn't he, it's she. ("No" to R, "Yes" to L)

5. I'll go with you, but not with him. (As you think, "I'll go with you," sign YOU and nod, "yes." As you think, "but not with him," sign IT-R and shake your head, "no.")

6. I see you and him do it, but not her. (Sign YOU and IT-R with your RH, nodding, "yes," then sign IT-L with your LH, shaking your head, "no.")

7. I don't do it, she does! (Attitudes: vehement denial, exasperation, anger, relief, etc.)

8. He doesn't do it!

9. I know for sure that you, he and she do it.

10. I would never do a thing like that.

The head movement affirms or negates a sign. The facial expression you use will depend upon how you feel about what you are signing. Students of Ameslan are often perplexed about how to ask questions in Ameslan. They often cannot perceive the difference between a simple declarative sentence, and an interrogative sentence. This difficulty arises from inexperience in reading the facial expressions, and the head movements. These features are often so subtle that they are missed by the untrained eye.

There are no set rules as to what facial expression, or which head movement the signer ought to use when asking a question. These are determined by the style of the signer. There are, however, some general patterns that you will frequently spot, which are common to questions.

In questions, the facial expression will usually incorporate the raised, or arched eyebrows. Sometimes only one eyebrow is arched, sometimes both are. Often the eyebrows will knit into a frown.

The head will often tilt, depending upon the nature of the question:

1. For simple, straightforward questions, the head tends to tilt forward.

2. For questions of a satirical, or skeptical nature, the head tends to tilt backward.

3. For questions of an intimate nature, or questions you are not sure you ought to ask, or questions of a pleading nature, the head tends to tilt to the side.

Bear in mind, these are only general patterns, they are not set, obligatory patterns.

EXERCISE 3

Do these questions in the same way you did the sentences in Exercise 2, except that here you should work on questioning facial expressions, and head tilts.

1. Are you the one?

2. So, you're the one, huh?

3. Now, aren't you really the one?

4. You mean me?

5. You think I'm the one? (Sign YOU, then ME.)

6. Now, would I do that?

7. Are you sure he does it? (Sign YOU, then IT-R)

8. Why me?

9. What! She's doing it now?

10. I do it all the time, do you? (Careful, the first part is an affirmative statement, only the "do you?" part is a question.)

If you really got into Exercises 2 and 3, you found that your shoulders were very much in the act. In fact, one very common device for asking questions is to shrug your shoulders, and hold your hands out, palms up.

EXERCISE 4

When you ask negative questions, remember to shake the head, "no," while making a questioning expression with your face, and the appropriate head tilt, and be sure you use your shoulders when it is appropriate.

1. You don't do it ever?

2. Are you sure you don't do it?

3. Are you trying to tell me that he doesn't know? (As you think, "Are you trying," sign, YOU; then think, "to tell me," sign, ME; then think, "that he doesn't know?" and sign IT-R-NEG. the "NEG." written as part of a sign name means to negate the sign by shaking your head.

4. I don't have to do it, do I?

5 He isn't telling her?

6. How am I supposed to know if you don't tell me?

7. You don't really do that, do you?

8. Don't you understand?

9. You aren't going to ask me, are you?

10. Why don't you tell me? (Try this one just shrugging your shoulders.)

NOTES

LESSON

BOY
boy

GIRL
girl, female

Sign these sentences, remembering to supply the facial expressions, head tilts and shoulder movements.

EXERCISE 5

I understand.
I don't understand.

I understand you.
I do not understand you.
I understand the boy.
I do not understand the boy.
I understand the girl.
I do not understand the girl.

The boy understands the girl.
The boy does not understand the girl.
Does the boy understand the girl?

The girl understands you.
The girl understands me.
Does the girl understand you?
Doesn't the girl understand me?

You understand me.
You do not understand me.
Do you understand?
Don't you understand?
You understand the boy.
You do not understand the boy.
Do you understand the boy?
Don't you understand the boy?
You understand the girl.
Do you understand the girl?
Don't you understand the girl?

UNDERSTAND
to understand or comprehend; to realize

The SEE sign has a characteristic which UNDERSTAND does not have. The SEE sign moves away from the signer towards the person or object which is seen. This movement of a sign towards the object is called directionality. We say that the sign is directional. It is critically important to grasp the significance of directionality.

SEE
to see, behold; sight, vision

S   "I see you."

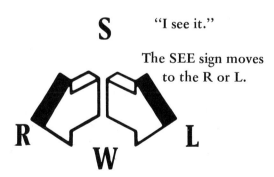

The SEE sign moves from the signer towards the watcher

W

S   "I see it."

The SEE sign moves to the R or L.

R   **L**
W

Since the sign moves toward the person or object which is seen, it is not necessary to point to the person or object.

"I see you," sign: ME SEE. The "you" is understood, because the SEE sign moves toward W.

"I see it," sign: ME SEE-R/L.

It is not necessary to sign, ME SEE YOU, or ME SEE-R/L IT-R/L. You may sign YOU, and IT-R/L in these sentences, but it is not necessary. When you do make signs like these, which are not mandatory, you generally do so to emphasize an idea. So, ME SEE YOU, would mean, "I see YOU!"

The SEE sign moves in only one direction (it is uni-directional), away from the signer. It cannot be reversed to move toward the signer. In order to sign, "You see me," you must sign, YOU SEE ME. The SEE sign is not moving toward the person ("me"), but rather away from the person, so you must sign, ME. Verb signs such as UNDERSTAND are called non-directional.

MAN
man, mankind, male

I see you.
I do not see you.
I see the man.
I do not see the man.
I see the woman.
I do not see the woman.

You see me.
You see the man.
You see the woman.
You see me.
You see the man.
You do not see the man.
You do not see the woman.

Do you see me ?
Do you see the man?
Does the woman see you?
Do you see the woman?
Does the woman see me?
Does the woman see the man?
Doesn't the man see you?
Doesn't the man see the woman.
Don't you see me?
Don't you see the man?
Don't you see the woman?

The man sees you.
The man sees me.
The man sees the woman.
The woman does not see you.
The woman does not see me.
The woman does not see the man.

When the SEE sign is tapped on the cheek several times, rather than moved outwards, the sign becomes an idiom. It is called LET'S-SEE. The meaning varies with the facial expression, the vigor with which you make the sign, and with the context of the statement. Here are some examples. Think these sentences to yourself as you make the LET'S SEE sign.

WOMAN
woman

1. I want to see.

2. Let me see.

3. Let's see what's in the box!

4. You'll see, you'll be sorry!

5. We'll see about it later.

12

HELP
help, assist, aid, render support

The HELP sign differs from the SEE sign in terms of its directionality. Whereas SEE may move only away from the signer (uni-directional), HELP may move away from the signer, towards the signer, and from R to L, or L to R (it is multi-directional).

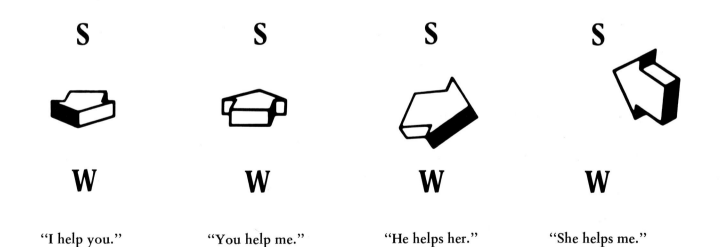

"I help you."   "You help me."   "He helps her."   "She helps me."

Since HELP, like SEE, moves toward its object, the object is not signed. Furthermore, since HELP moves from the subject, the subject need not be signed either.

In none of these examples is it necessary to sign ME, YOU, or IT-R/L, because the direction in which the sign moves tells you who is giving to whom.

"I help you." Sign: HELP (The sign moves from S, so I need not sign ME. It moves toward W, so I need not sign YOU.)

"You help me." Sign: HELP W—S (HELP moves from "you"---the watcher---to "me"---the signer.)

"I help him." Sign: HELP R.

"You help him." Sign: HELP W—R (The sign begins in the area near W, then moves to the R area.)

"He helps you." Sign: HELP R—W (The sign begins in the R area and moves toward W.)

"He helps her." Sign: HELP R—L (The sign begins in R and moves to L.)

"She helps me." Sign: HELP L—S (The sign moves from L to S.)

FATHER
father, dad, pop, papa

EXERCISE 7

I help you.
I don't help you.
I help father.
I don't help father.
I help mother.
I don't help mother.

You help me.
You help father.
You help mother.
You don't help me.
You don't help father.
You don't help mother.
Do you help me?
Do you help father?
Do you help mother?
Don't you help me?
Don't you help father?
Don't you help mother?

Father helps you.
Father helps me.
Father helps mother.

MOTHER
mother, mom, mommy, mama

HELP W-S FATHER?
HELP W-R FATHER?
YOU HELPS-W FATHER?

how

where was it stood

14

Mother doesn't help you .
Mother doesn't help me .
Mother doesn't help father .

Does father help you?
Does father help me?
Does father help mother?

Doesn't mother help you?
Doesn't mother help me?
Doesn't mother help father?

Many verb signs in Ameslan are non-directional, uni-directional, or multi-directional, so you must learn not only how to make the sign, but also when to move it, and in what direction to move it. This quality of directionality is one of Ameslan's most distinctive characteristics, therefore be sure you understand how it works.

LOVE
love, adore, cherish, regard with affection

TELL
tell, relate

GIVE
give, donate, present, bestow

EXERCISE 8

Go through Exercises 5, 6, and 7, substituting the LOVE, TELL, and GIVE signs in the sentences where they make sense.

15

NEW SIGNS TO REVIEW

BOY	GIVE
FATHER	HELP
GIRL	LOVE
MAN	SEE
WOMAN	TELL
MOTHER	UNDERSTAND

LESSON

Signs are often reproduced in a sentence. To avoid confusion, the word "repeat" will mean that a sign is done two or three times. Example: GIVE, GIVE, GIVE is called repeating the GIVE sign. Instead of writing GIVE three times, we use a numerical superscript: GIVE^3. The meaning of GIVE^3 is: "I give to you a lot," or, "I'm always giving to you."

When a sign is reproduced later in the sentence, it will be called "copying." Example: ME SEE-R HELP R—W ME. It may be compared to "I see him help you, I do," or, "It is I who sees him help you." When the pointing signs, ME, YOU, IT-R/L (and from now on to be referred to as the indexing signs, or just plain indexing) are the subjects of a sentence, they are often copied at the end of the sentence.

"I love you." Sign: ME LOVE YOU ME.

"You see me." Sign: YOU SEE ME YOU.

"He gives to me." Sign: GIVE-R—S IT-R.

Sometimes copying is for emphasis. When that is the case, there will be appropriate facial expression, and the indexing will be made with differing degrees of vigor.

It is not mandatory that the indexing signs be copied at the end of the sentence, but it is a very common thing to see.

Another characteristic of indexing signs is their frequent appearance following a noun sign.

"The woman loves you." Sign: WOMAN IT-L LOVE YOU. (Ameslan has no articles--"a," "an," and "the.")

"The woman sees me." Sign: WOMAN IT-L SEE ME.

"The woman gives to him." Sign: WOMAN IT-L GIVE-L—R.

Row Give-L-R ?

This use of indexing seems to function as a definite article, or a demonstrative pronoun, "the woman," "that woman," "this woman," as opposed to any woman in general. For example, WOMAN LOVE YOU, without indexing, could mean, "Women love you."

EXERCISE 9

1. The boy helps the girl to understand.

2. The boy gives many things to the girl.

3. Men love that woman.

4. I am telling you to give to the girl.

5. Do you see the girl help me?

6. I keep telling you to help the boy.

7. I don't understand this woman.

8. Are you telling the man to help me?

9. He sees you tell the woman to help me.

10. Don't you understand the girl?

LESSON

In Lesson 4, the word "spatialization" was used with reference to the indexing signs. Lest you presume that spatialization means merely pointing, we need to expand the meaning. Spatialization means:

1. To place objects and events in specific areas in the space around you by indexing them.

2. To make the sign for an object or event in a specific area, or toward a specific area.

Spatialization makes it easier to see the relationships of the objects and events to each other. It also makes it easier for the signer to refer back to them.

To illustrate the above, suppose you want to sign something involving four persons: two women, W, and S. W and S are spatialized by their physical presence. It remains then to spatialize the two women. You may do this in three ways:

1. Using the technique described in No. 1 above: WOMAN IT-L//WOMAN IT-R. If you use your LH for the woman to your left, and your RH for the woman to your right, you further reinforce the spatialization. (The "//" indicates a pause, or the end of a statement.)

2. Using the technique described in No. 2 above: sign WOMAN with your LH, and at the same time tilt your body slightly to L, focusing your eyes to L; then sign, WOMAN with your RH, while tilting and focusing to R. This is written WOMAN-L, WOMAN-R.

3. Combine both 1 and 2.

Now using one of these three ways, sign the sentence: "The women see you." First, spatialize the two women, then sign SEE. Then if you wish to say, "They understand you," all you need do is refer back to the areas where you spatialized the two women, LH IT-L// RH IT-R UNDERSTAND YOU. The LH and RH indexing would be done simultaneously.

From then on, whatever else you wanted to say about the two women would be done merely by indexing the areas they occupy.

BOOK
[1] book; [2] open the book (close the book is simply closing the palms back together)

Practice spatializing the BOOK sign:

1. Make it in front and close to you. This implies the book is near you. (BOOK)

2. Make it in front, but closer to W. The book is near W. (BOOK-W)

3. Make it in the R area. The book is in that area. (BOOK-R)

4. Do the same for the L area, and the meaning is the same. (BOOK-L)

When the noun sign is written without any spatialization symbols (BOOK, as opposed to BOOK-W/L/R), it means the object is spatialized comfortably in front of you, in "zero" space.

Ameslan usually follows the English order of subject-verb-object, particularly if the object is animate: "The boy loves the girl," (BOY-R LOVE GIRL-L). If the verb sign is directional, however, the subject-verb-object order may be altered: "The boy helps the girl," ([1.] BOY-R HELP R-L GIRL-L, or [2] GIRL-L BOY-R HELP R-L). The direction HELP moves shows clearly which is the subject and which is the object.

If the object is inanimate, the order of subject-verb-object may be departed from freely: "I love books," ([1] ME LOVE BOOK, [2] BOOK ME LOVE, [3] LOVE ME BOOK, [4] LOVE BOOK ME, etc.).

The object may come before the verb if:

1. the object is inanimate; or,
2. the verb sign is directional.

If in doubt, follow the subject-verb-object pattern, and you will rarely be wrong.

When there is an object, and an indirect object, Ameslan usually follows the subject-verb-direct object-indirect object order: "I give the book to the boy," (ME GIVE-R BOOK-R BOY-R IT-R). However, because of spatialization, and sign directionality other orders are possible:

ME BOOK GIVE-R BOY-R IT-R
BOY-R IT-R BOOK GIVE-R ME

The sentence, "I see the man give the book to the woman," may be signed:

1. ME SEE-R MAN-R//GIVE R–L BOOK-L WOMAN-L;

2. ME SEE-R MAN-R BOOK-R//GIVE R–L WOMAN-L;

3. MAN-R WOMAN-L//ME SEE-R BOOK-R GIVE R–L;

4. MAN-R WOMAN-L BOOK-R//GIVE R–L SEE-R ME;

5. ME SEE-R MAN-R//GIVE R–L WOMAN-L BOOK-L.

20

All five sentences are acceptable in Ameslan, however, sentence five is unusual because the verb and direct object are not together. Ameslan resists this separation, preferring that the direct object be either immediately before or after the verb.

None of the five sentences is ambiguous due to the spatialization of MAN on the right, WOMAN on the left, BOOK on the right and left, and the directionality of SEE and GIVE.

PENCIL, or WRITE
[1] a writing instrument of any kind,
i.e., pencil, pen, crayon, chalk, etc.,
[2] write, writing

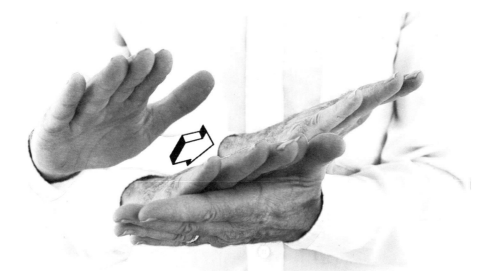

PAPER
paper

NEW SIGNS TO REVIEW :

        BOOK

        PENCIL or WRITE

        PAPER

EXERCISE 10

Sign each sentence in as many different subject-verb-object orders as you can.

1. I see the pencil.

2. Do you see the paper?

3. I'm always giving you paper.

4. Tell the girl to give the woman the book.

5. The boy tells me that he loves that book.

6. The woman tells me that she loves books.

7. I want to see the paper.

8. I tell the boy to tell her to give you paper and pencil. (There is a sign for "and," but it would not be used here.)

9. I understand this book, not that one.

10. You give me the book, and I give it to the man.

LESSON

Ameslan is a highly contextual language. That is, many meanings are deduced from the context of a conversation, and from the context of a situation. We must, for example, look for contextual clues to tell us whether an action is in the past or the future. Suppose I want to sign, "I saw you yesterday." There is no way to alter SEE so that it means "saw." Rather we take our cue from the sign, YESTERDAY.

YESTERDAY
yesterday, the previous day, the day
before

23

You must sign, YESTERDAY ME SEE. SEE does not change, instead we look to YESTERDAY to give us the contextual cue we need to know when the act took place.

Signs like YESTERDAY, which specify the time of an event, are called time-indicators, or time adverbials. Many time-indicators come at the very beginning of a statement, thus, we know that everything which follows the time-indicator occurred during the time indicated by the sign.

TOMORROW
tomorrow, the next day, the following day, the day after

The sentence, "I'll see you tomorrow," is signed: TOMORROW ME SEE.

WILL is not strictly a time-indicator. Although it does refer to future time, it also conveys a person's intention to do something in future time. As such, it belongs to a group of signs which express emotional reactions, attitudes, states of being, etc. These kinds of signs generally follow the verb,

rather than come at the beginning. Thus, if you sign, TOMORROW ME SEE WILL, it means that tomorrow I intend to see you, that I will make every effort to see you, etc.

WILL
[1] future; [2] will, would, shall; [3] intention to do something

EXERCISE 11

Translate and practice. Remember to put the time-indicators YESTERDAY and TOMORROW at the beginning.

1. Yesterday I told you to help the man.

2. Did you see the woman yesterday?

3. I won't see you tomorrow. (sign: TOMORROW ME SEE-NEG. The WILL expresses positive intention, and is rarely negated. There are other signs that could be used here which you will learn later.)

4. Did the man tell you yesterday to give the book to the woman?

5. I'll tell the woman tomorrow.

6. Didn't the man give the woman the book yesterday?

7. Yesterday I didn't understand, tomorrow I will. (Be sure there is a strong contrast of head movement between the negative and positive portions.)

8. Will you help me tomorrow?

9. Yesterday, I gave the book to the woman: she'll give it to you tomorrow.

10. You told the man yesterday to give me the book, will he?

MORNING
morning

DAY
day, daytime

NOON
noon, noontime, at noon, mid-day

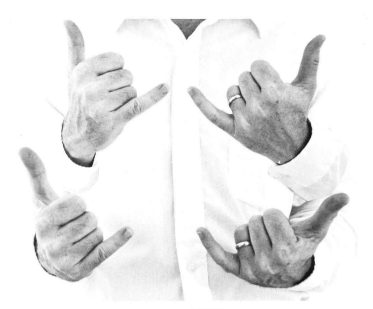

NOW
[1] at the moment, now, present; [2] today

When YESTERDAY is combined with NIGHT, it means, "last night," or "the previous night," or "the night before." There is another, more common way to sign, "last night," which you will learn later.

When NOW is combined with DAY (NOW DAY), it means "today," or "this day." When it is combined with MORNING, it means, "this morning;" NOW NOON means "this noon," or "today at noon;" NOW AFTERNOON means "this afternoon;" NOW NIGHT means "tonight." Often NOW by itself means "today."

NIGHT
night, evening, night time

AFTERNOON
afternoon

EXERCISE 12

Translate and practice.

1. I will see you this morning.

2. I will see the man in the morning. (Suppose it is night when you sign this.)

3. Did I give you the book last night?

4. Yesterday morning you told me that you would give me the paper.

5. I'll see the girl at noon today.

6. You help me this afternoon, I'll help you tomorrow afternoon.

7. The woman will tell you tomorrow night.

8. The man told the boy this morning that you would help the woman tonight.

9. Last night I didn't understand, today I do.

10. Will you give me a pencil tonight?

11. Didn't you see the man last night?

12. Give me the book now! (NOW! comes last here, because it is being used in an emphatic command. In other words, it is expressing a strong emotional reaction.)

13. Tell the woman I'll help her.

14. Did you understand the man last night?

15. I saw the woman give the book to the man yesterday at noon.

NEW SIGNS TO REVIEW:

AFTERNOON

MORNING

DAY

NOON

NIGHT

NOW

WILL

TOMORROW

YESTERDAY

NOTES

LESSON 7

In Lesson 6 you learned how to place events in the past by using the time-indicator, YESTERDAY. It may be called a "specific" time-indicator, because it specifies how far in the past the event took place, i.e., "yesterday." Now you are going to learn two time-indicator signs that refer to an unspecified time in the past.

FINISH
[1] to indicate that an action is over with, done, completed; [2] already; [3] to indicate sufficiency of an action, e.g., "That's enough!" or "Stop it!"; [4] to indicate that when one event was completed, another followed in sequence, e.g., "After we ate, we left," EAT FINISH//GO-R//

PAST
[1] to indicate that an action took place, is in the past; [2] past, previously, before, ago; [3] when combined with nouns, e.g., PAST NIGHT, it means, "last night," or "one night ago"

These two signs set the time of an action in the past, but they do not specify exactly how far in the past. The sentence, ME SEE FINISH, simply means, "I saw you," or as we often say in English, "I did see you." The sentence, ME SEE PAST, means, "I saw you before (sometime in the past)."

FINISH simply means that the action of the verb is past, over with (except in the case of questions). There are many ways to say it in English, but only one way to sign it in Ameslan. For example, TELL FINISH or FINISH TELL may be translated as: "I told you," "I did tell you," "I already told you," "I have told you," etc.

In question form, FINISH asks if the action is past. For example, TELL? FINISH? means: "Did I tell you?" "Did I already tell you?" "Have I told you?" "Have I told you already?"

The FINISH and PAST signs may follow or come before the verb, but FINISH tends to follow the verb. Example: "I did give you the book." Sign: BOOK FINISH GIVE// or BOOK GIVE FINISH//. Often FINISH is added for additional emphasis: "I gave you the book last night," signed: PAST NIGHT BOOK GIVE//FINISH//. FINISH is not necessary here, because PAST NIGHT tells us the event is over with, but it does add an additional touch of emphasis.

EXERCISE 13

Translate and practice.

1. He gave me a pencil.

2. Did you give her the paper?

3. Did the boy previously tell you to help me?

4. I saw the woman tell the boy to help her.

5. He loved her once, but not now. (Since "once" here implies that he loved her sometime in the past, use PAST. The "but not now," is signed, NOW-NEG.)

6. I have already told you.

7. Has he finished helping her?

8. She already told me last night.

9. I have seen the book already.

10. Had you seen the book before?

The FINISH sign is used when reporting a sequence of events. In a sentence such as, "When he had given me the book, I helped him," there are two events reported. The sequence is: [1] his giving me the book, and [2] my helping him. So it is signed: BOOK-R GIVE-R–S FINISH//HELP-S–R. The signed sentence could also be translated: "After he gave me the book, I helped him." and "He gave me the book, then I helped him."

Compare the two sentences:

"After he gave me the book, I helped him."
"I helped him after he gave me the book."

They are identical in meaning. Now compare these two sentences:

BOOK-R GIVE-R–S FINISH//HELP-S–R//
HELP-R FINISH//BOOK-R GIVE-R–S//

They are opposite in meaning. English can express the same thought two different ways, Ameslan can do it in only one way. The reason for this is found in a very important principle of Ameslan sentence structure.

The events reported in a signed sentence follow, in general, the same sequence in which they actually occurred. In the above example, you first relate the giving of the book, then the helping, because that is how it actually happened. If you get the signs out of sequence to the actual facts, as we did in the second Ameslan sentence above, the meaning is totally reversed.

This characteristic of the language results from the application of the time-sequence principle. Whenever you translate an English sentence into Ameslan, always look first to see if the events are arranged in the correct time sequence, the chronological order in which they occurred. If they are not, rearrange the English until the events do correspond to that order, then translate the sentence into Ameslan.

As a person speaks, pausing and rythm are essential for clarification of meaning, and for adding nuances to the meanings of the words. Pausing and rhythm are as essential in signing as in speak-

ing, so you must learn where to pause, and when to speed up or slow down, or change the rigor with which the sign is made. This knowledge is gained primarily through experience, but an attempt will be made to indicate pauses, and ends of statements with the symbols "//."

Example: SEE FINISH//BOOK GIVE//

Notice, also, that this sentence illustrates how FINISH is used only once, following SEE, and not repeated after GIVE. One FINISH is sufficient to put both verb signs in the past: "After I saw you, I gave you the book," "When I saw you, I gave you the book," "I saw you, then I gave you the book." However, the statement could refer to future time, "After I see you, I'll give you the book," "I'll give you the book when I see you," "I'll see you, then give you the book." Without more context than we have here, it is impossible to tell. Naturally, the question would be answered immediately by the addition of WILL.

NEW SIGNS TO REVIEW:

FINISH

PAST

EXERCISE 14

Translate and practice.

1. After I saw you, I gave you the book.

2. When he had helped her, she told him that she loved him. (Do not repeat FINISH after the TELL sign, it is not necessary, because the FINISH sign after the HELP sign puts it all in the past.)

3. Give me the book, then I will help you.

4. You understood after I told you.

5. I saw you after you gave her the book.

6. I told her to help you after you told him to help me.

7. Will you help me after you give him the book?

8. When he saw you give me the book, he told her to help you.

9. He gave her the book yesterday, then this morning she gave it back.

10. Did you tell him to give her the book, then to help me?

11. Had you already given her the book last night?

LESSON

In Lesson 7 we touched briefly on the time-sequence principle. In this lesson we shall go into it in more detail.

WORK
employment, job, work (verb and noun)

HOME
home

HOME
home

HOME
home

34

EAT
[1] eat; [2] food

BED
[1] bed; [2] go to bed, go to sleep

ACROSS
[1] go across, cross over; [2] across, over; go or pass over; [3] after

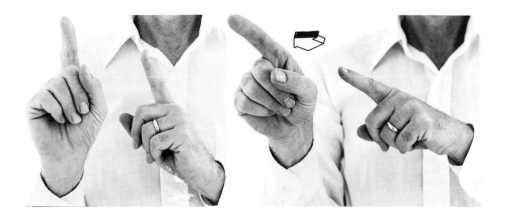

GO-TO
[1] go, with emphasis on going to a specific place; [2] when repeated it means "to go regularly or often"

Suppose you wish to say in English, "I'm going home after work." You could just as well say, "After work, I'm going home." Both statements are grammatically correct.

In Ameslan, however, there is a strong tendency to follow the natural order of events:WORK FINISH //GO-TO R HOME//, or AFTER WORK FINISH// GO-TO R HOME// (AFTER is generally followed by FINISH, though it can appear alone). It would be less common to sign: GO-TO R HOME AFTER WORK FINISH//.

The time-sequence principle is the major principle in governing the order of signs. You must learn to think in this pattern before you express yourself in signs. Suppose you wanted to tell a deaf person, "I was excited by the gorgeous colors of the sunrise this morning." Now you must first re-arrange your thoughts, placing the events in the "real life" sequence. First, think: "When did it happen?" (this morning), "What came next?" (the sunrise), "Describe it" (the goregous colors), "Then what happened?" (it excited me). The statement now runs: "This morning the sun rose and the gorgeous colors excited me." Now you are ready to put it into signs.

SUNRISE
[1] sunrise, dawn; [2] to oversleep

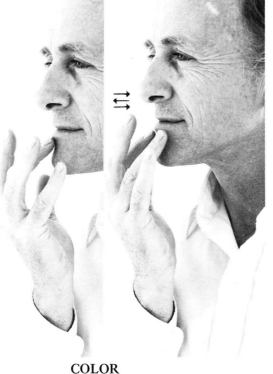

COLOR
color, colored

CLEAR
[1] clear, bright; [2] clearly, obviously

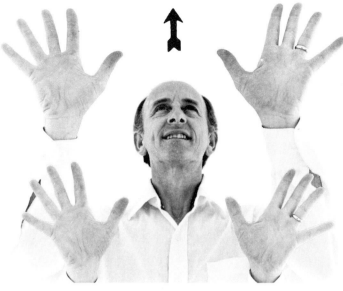

RAYS
rays of light

One way would be: NOW MORNING//SUNRISE //COLOR RAYS (moving U)//THRILL ME//. There are, of course, other signs one could use, but they would still be arranged in accordance with the time-sequence principle.

EXERCISE 15

Re-arrange the following so that they are consistent with the time-sequence principle. You need not be concerned that you use exactly the same words, just get the ideas in the correct order. Also, do not be concerned at this point how to sign the sentences.

Example: "What a relief that my car had nothing seriously wrong with it." Re-write: "My car had nothing wrong with it. What a relief!" The logic here is that you could not feel the relief until first you found out that your car had nothing wrong with it.

EXERCISE 15

1. We had lots of fun then, even though we had no automobiles to take us anywhere.

2. I like nothing so much as a tall, cool glass of iced tea when I come in all sweaty from mowing the lawn on a hot summer day.

THRILL
[1] thrill, thrilling, excite, excitement;
[2] idiomatically: "What's up?" "What's wrong?"

3. I hate to get out of bed on cold, rainy mornings, but once I'm up, I'm okay.

4. Isn't it odd how we seem unable to run fast in our dreams, but rather keep falling down, or else run in slow motion as if our shoes were made of lead.

5. I finally got to England last summer, something I had always wanted to do.

6. If ever you get to London, be sure to visit Westminster Cathedral. I saw it a few years ago and was immensely impressed with it. There are many famous people buried there, and I felt as if I had met them just by seeing their graves.

7. "Oh! I'm terribly sorry!" he said, then he picked up the packages strewn all over the floor, which was the result of him bumping into me.

8. Ivan the Terrible ordered St. Basil's Cathedral to be built during the 16th century in honor of Russia's liberation from the Tartars, which occurred in the 15th century. Mocking the austerity of the martial par-

ades, and the spartan simplicity of Lenin's tomb, St. Basil's sits on Red Square looking as if it had been sculptured in chocolate, vanilla, and pistachio ice cream. (With apologies to Jack Smith of the LOS ANGELES TIMES.)

9. We were all greatly concerned at the news that Walter had been struck on the head by a falling tree last week. He had been out tramping through the woods at the time, and had taken shelter under a tree, when a thunderstorm blew up. Lightning struck the tree, and Walter was hit by one of the lower branches of the tree as it fell.

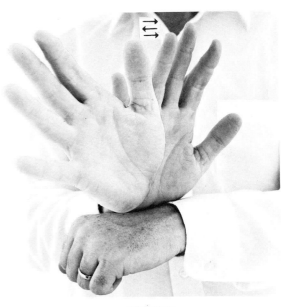

MOVIE
motion pictures, movie, cinema

With statements of only three or less signs in length, you need not be greatly concerned with the sign order. For example, the statement, "I've seen the movie," may be signed:

MOVIE SEE FINISH	SEE FINISH MOVIE
MOVIE FINISH SEE	FINISH SEE MOVIE
SEE MOVIE FINISH	FINISH MOVIE SEE

With such short statements, it does not seem to matter in what order they are signed. Naturally, there are some exceptions to this, which will be taken up later.

NEW SIGNS TO REVIEW

BED	ACROSS	HOME	SUNRISE
CLEAR	COLOR	MOVIE	THRILL
EAT	GO-TO	RAYS	WORK

GOOD
[1] good, well; [2] thank you, thanks

VERY GOOD

DIALOGUE

Memorize and practice with another person.

A: Good morning!
B: Hello!
A: I'm glad to see you.
B: How are you?
A: Fine, how are you?
B: Lousy, I've been sick.
A: Do you feel better now?
B: Yes, thank you.
A: Goodbye, I have to go now.
B: Good night, take it easy.

EXPLANATION

1. "Good morning!"

When the RH is slapped sharply against the LH, the meaning is, "very good!" Often, the LH is not used at all. When combining GOOD and MORNING, the LH is not used to make the GOOD sign, but is poised ready to make MORNING. The RH moves smoothly from GOOD into MORNING.

If you are holding something with your LH, you may sign GOOD MORNING with just the RH alone. Practice that.

Your facial expression ought to be pleasant.

HELLO
a gesture used in greetings and partings

2. "Hello!"

Like "Aloha" and "Shalom," it is used to greet someone, and also used when parting.

3. "I'm glad to see you."

The "I'm" is not signed, since it is clearly understood who is glad.

The SEE moves toward W, meaning, "I see you," so the "you" is not signed. You could sign YOU if you wished to emphasize "you," but it is not necessary. Also, the "I" part of "I see you" is not signed because it is understood as well.

Sign: GLAD SEE// or SEE GLAD//. If you wished to emphasize it, sign: GLAD SEE YOU!//

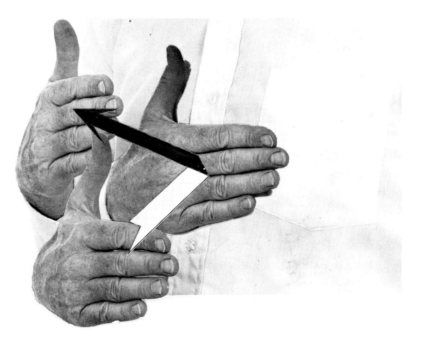

GLAD
glad, happy, happiness

4. "How are you?"

Ameslan has no "to be" verb. Thus you do not have a sign for "are."

There is a sign called TRUE...

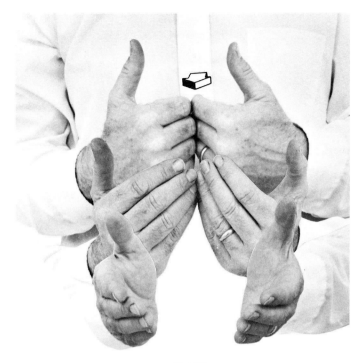

HOW
how, in what way or manner

TRUE
[1] expresses the idea of "isness," the reality of a thing; emphasizes the existence of something; [2] true, truth, real surely, certain, certainly

... that may be used, but it is an emphatic sign. It stresses the reality of something. If you use it in this sentence, it will mean, "How are you, really and truly?"

Sign: HOW? YOU?// (The question mark written as part of the sign means to make the sign with a questioning expression on your face. It is not a mark of punctuation, but rather a cue to you as to what type facial expression you should use.)

5. "Fine! How are you?"

FINE
[1] fine, very well, good; [2] O.K.

The FINE sign is usually done as shown. However, you may alter or inflect the sign to get greater intensities. The fingers may wriggle; the hand moves out (or in) in a sharp movement; both hands may make the sign; both hands, fingers wriggling, move up

41

the chest, then outward sharply. These alterations express such ideas as, "Great!" "Terrific!" "Superb!" "Fantastic!", etc.

The "How are you?" would not be signed, merely use the YOU sign with a questioning expression.

Sign: FINE//YOU?// (There is a change of facial expression here from looking fine to questioning.)

6. "Lousy! I've been sick."

LOUSY
lousy, no good, terrible, very bad, awful

SICK
sick, sickness, ill, disease

The SICK sign is usually made with just the RH as shown, but sometimes you will see the LH placed on the stomach along with the RH on the forehead.

UP-TILL-NOW
[1] indicates that a condition or state of being has existed from some time in the past up until the present, or the recent past; [2] since, been, for

The UP-TILL-NOW sign is used to refer to an event that began in the past and has continued up to the present, or up until just recently. It usually comes before the thing to which it refers, but it may often follow it.

Sign: LOUSY//UP-TILL-NOW SICK// or LOUSY//SICK UP-TILL-NOW.

7. "Do you feel better now?"

Ameslan has no sign comparable to the word "do" when it is used as it is here. Actually the word as used is devoid of meaning. You could just as easily say, "You feel better now?"

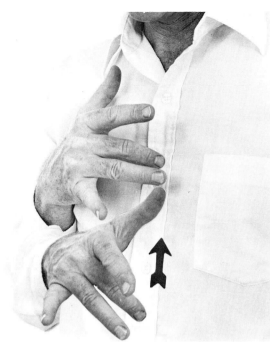

FEEL
to feel or sense either physically or emotionally

The FEEL sign would usually be stroked only once up the chest in this sentence. If the stroke is repeated with the proper facial expression, the meaning becomes, "I have a feeling that....." "I have a hunch that....."

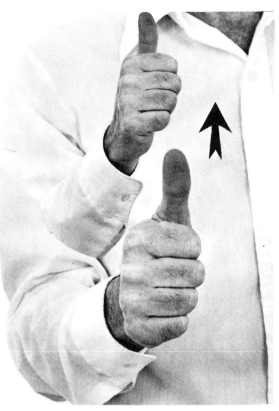

COMPARATIVE or FOREMOST
[1] the comparative marker is a one handed MOST, when it follows an adjective it produces the comparative form; [2] when used with nouns, or used alone, it means uppermost, foremost, most important, major

MOST
most, nearly all, a majority of

BETTER
actually a blend of GOOD and COMPARATIVE

43

The comparative marker always follows the adjective. In this case, start the sign GOOD, then move quickly into the marker.

English has only two degrees of intensification of adjectives, comparative and superlative (good, better, best). Ameslan has several degrees. Already you saw how FINE can be elevated to greater intensities by altering the sign itself. Now use FINE plus the comparative marker, each time moving the marker higher and more vigorously. You ought to be able to perceive at least three degrees of intensity. Now, if instead of using the comparative marker, you switch to the MOST sign.

You can get two or three higher levels of intensity. "Best" is often signed: GOOD MOST.

The facial expression and the vigor with which the sign is made, add the various nuances and colors to the meaning of the adjective.

Sign: [NOW?] FEEL? BETTER? NOW?// (When a sign is placed within brackets, it means that the sign is optional.)

The NOW may come first or last, or even in both positions. Remember that in statements of three or fewer signs, the order will vary.

8. "Yes, thank you."

The THANKS sign is made identically to GOOD. Sometimes THANKS will move until the hand is parallel to the floor palm up. For greater emphasis, use both hands. The meaning then becomes, "gratitude," "appreciation." Sometimes THANKS is used for, "You're welcome," as well as, "Thank you."

Sign: YES//GOOD//

Always nod the head when signing YES.

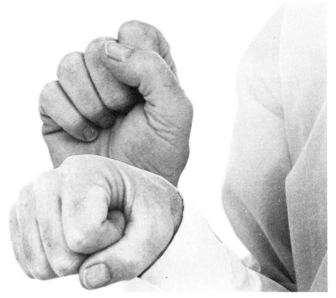

YES
the affirmative sign, yes

9. "Goodbye, I have to go now."

You may use this sign or the HELLO sign.

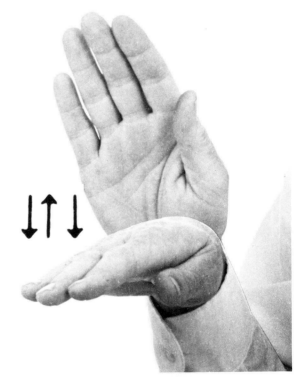

GOODBYE
a gesture used for parting, or to wave to someone

44

MUST
[1] expresses obligation or necessity; must, necessary, need, need to, have to, got to; [2] should, ought to, supposed to

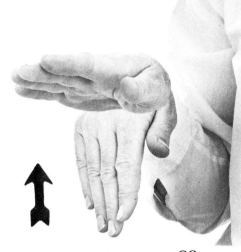

GO
go, with the emphasis on going away from a place, leaving

When meaning No. 1 is desired, make MUST with one movement downward, the sharpness with which you make the sign determines the degree of obligation. In other words, for "I have to go," the movement is soft. If you are pressed for time, however, and your friend is begging you not to go, but it is imperative for you to leave, then make MUST with a larger and quicker movement.

This sign differs from GO-TO only in emphasis. GO emphasizes going away from a place, while GO-TO emphasizes going to a place.

Sign:

GOODBYE //[MUST] GO-R NOW MUST.//
HELLO

(When two or more signs may be used, they will be written one above the other.)

When meaning No. 2 is desired, make MUST with two gentle "taps" downward.

The MUST sign generally comes at the end of a statement.

10. "Good night, take it easy."

The GOOD and NIGHT should flow together almost as if they were one sign.

SELF
[1] a pronoun marker comparable to the English "self" (myself, yourself, etc.); [2] idiom meaning, "Take care of yourself," "Take it easy," "Hello!" "goodbye"

The SELF sign is directional. If moved back against S's chest, it means, "myself;" toward W, "yourself;" R/L, "himself," "herself," "itself." Often SELF replaces indexing, or is used with indexing for added emphasis.

SELF is also used idiomatically to mean, "Be good to yourself."

Sign: GOOD NIGHT//SELF
              HELLO
              GOODBYE

ADDITIONAL VOCABULARY

As you can see, these two signs are the reverse of GO-TO and GO. Use COME HERE when you wish to communicate the idea of someone coming to the place being discussed. Use COME to give the command to someone, "Come here!" "Come on!"

COME
the reverse of GO, used only in giving the commands, "Come!" "Come here!"

COME-HERE
the reverse of GO-TO, meaning to come from someplace to where you are at that moment

NEW SIGNS TO REVIEW:

BETTER	FEEL	GOODBYE	MUST
COME	FINE	HELLO	SELF
COME-HERE	GLAD	HOW	SICK
GO	LOUSY	TRUE	COMPARATIVE
YES	GOOD	MOST	UP-TILL-NOW
YES			VERY-GOOD

NOTES

EXERCISE 16

Translate into Ameslan. Remember first to check the time-sequence. If the material does not follow the correct sequence, revise it until the order is correct before you translate into Ameslan. Also, remember the pauses.

1. I went home yesterday morning after I saw you.

2. I told you I felt sick last night. I'm better this morning.

3. See you tomorrow, I'm going home now.

   (When NOW is not combined with DAY, NIGHT, MORNING, or AFTERNOON, it will generally come at the end of a statement. This sentence, for example, is signed TOMORROW SEE, GO HOME NOW. It acts somewhat like a command to start an action. In that capacity, you state the action first, then say that it is to be done "now.")

4. I need to see you tomorrow.

5. You've got to go, right now!

6. I felt better after he gave me the paper.

7. The man was happy to see the woman yesterday afternoon.

8. That is such a good book!

9. How will you give her the pencil?

10. Do you really feel terrible?

11. Today I feel terrific!

12. He has been going to her regularly.

13. I enjoy most going to the movies.

14. **I have a hunch he will tell you today.**

15. **Did you come here last night?**

16. You really ought to help him.

17. I already told you that I love you.

18. I don't understand this book.

19. Did you thank her?

20. I'll tell you tonight, I have to go to work now.

21. When the boy gave the girl the book, she was happy.

22. I'll be glad to help you.

NOTES

LESSON **10**

DIALOGUE

Memorize and practice with two other people.

A: Let's you and I practice signing.

B: Fine, no speaking, just signing.

A: What did you do last night?

B: Studied a little, then watched TV. What did you do?

A: I visited a deaf friend. We watched a captioned film.

B: (To C) Hi! What's up?

C: Nothing. Who's that? (Indexing to A)

B: Haven't you two met?

A: I think I met you once before, but I can't remember.

C: Are you deaf?

B: No, he's/she's hearing. His/Her name is Art/Amy, signed .... His/Her name is Sam/Sue, signed....... .

A&C: Glad to meet you.

C: Your name is Bob/Bev, but what's your sign?

B: (Shows name-sign.)

A: Let's go to the snack bar for coffee.

B&C: All right.

EXPLANATION

1. "Let's you and I practice signing."

LET
to give permission, allow, let

"Let's do....." is an English expression which is used to suggest something, rather than asking for permission to do something. In this sentence, A is not asking for permission, but is suggesting, therefore, LET would not be used here.

For "you and I" you may index, YOU ME, or use the WE-2 sign.

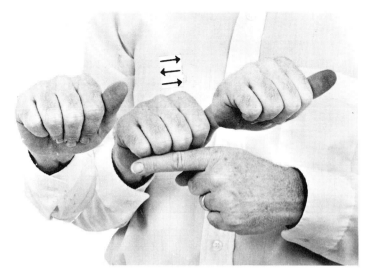

PRACTICE
practice, rehearse, drill, training

WE-2
we two, the two of us, you and I

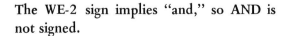

AND
and

SIGN
sign language, sign (verb and noun)

The WE-2 sign implies "and," so AND is not signed.

When the time-sequence principle does not seem to apply in helping you to determine the sign order, look next for concrete vs. abstract ordering. In general, Ameslan will put concrete things before abstract things. In this sentence, SIGN is more concrete than PRACTICE. You can see and touch a sign, but "practice" has no concrete identity. In this three-sign sentence, however, you may place the signs in whatever order you like, but to get you into the habit of thinking Ameslan:

Sign: WE-2 SIGN PRACTICE//

Facial expression is sort of asking a question, but encouraging B to say, "Yes."

2. "Fine, no speaking, just signing."

NO
[1] used to answer a question negatively, e.g., "No thank you;" [2] used to deny to someone something they want

NO is used primarily to answer a question in the negative.

If, for example, you wish to sign: "I told him to give me the paper, but he refused,"

one way would be: ME TELL-R PAPER-R GIVE R–S// IT-R NO (Towards S) //. The hand is turned so that the NO sign is made toward S. The NO sign may never be used to express the idea of "none," "not any," "nothing." In sentence two above, "no" means "not any," so use the NONE sign.

NONE
not any, none, nothing

Negative signs generally follow the thing which they negate. Always shake the head when making a sign of negation.

SPEAK
[1] the act of vocalizing; say, speak, speech; [2] used to refer to hearing persons, or schools for hearing children, i.e., public schools

ONLY
[1] only; [2] someone, something,
some (as in someday, sometime)

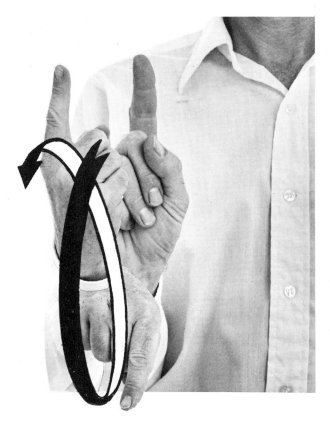

ONLY-ONE
one of a kind, unique, just one

In this sentence, "just" means "only" ("...no speaking, only signing"), so we would use the ONLY sign. If you want to be more emphatic, use the ONLY ONE sign. Both ONLY and ONLY ONE generally follow the thing to which they refer. This complies with putting the more concrete (SIGN) before the less concrete (ONLY).

Sign: FINE! SPEAK NONE //SIGN ONLY
//SIGN ONLY-ONE

The exclamation point written as part of a sign name (FINE!) is not a mark of punctuation, but a cue for you to make a facial expression of excitement, strong agreement, surprise, horror, etc., whatever is in keeping with the situation.

3. "What did you do last night?"

First, re-arrange for time-sequence: "Last night you did what?" We also re-arrange to put the interrogative "what?" at the end. Ameslan almost always does this . We also got rid of that troublesome "did" that means nothing, but we kept the "do" which does mean something.

WHAT
what?

54

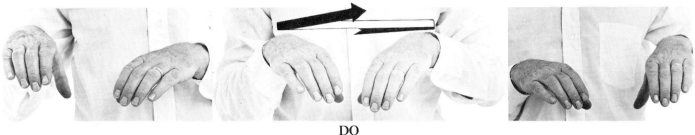

DO
to do, act, perform

DO is used only to indicate an action, a doing of some sort.

WHAT-SHRUG
what?

Both WHAT and WHAT-SHRUG mean the same thing, but the WHAT-SHRUG is much more common.

Sign: PAST NIGHT DO WHAT-SHRUG YOU?// (Final indexing is very, very common, so get used to it.)

4. "Studied a little, then watched TV. What did you do?"

STUDY
study

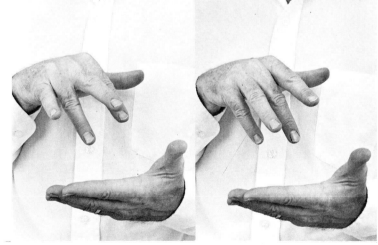

STUDY
study

Both signs mean the same thing, use either one.

55

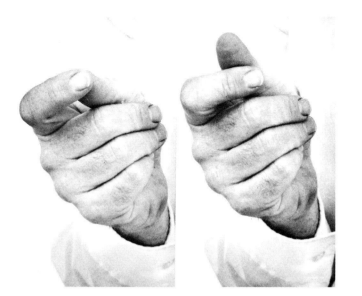

LITTLE
not much, little bit, small amount

This sign has to do only with quantities, amounts, not with size.

You would not use it when referring to, "a little boy," for example. There are other signs for "little" when size is meant.

Unlike SEE which is uni-directional, i.e., moves away from S toward W or IT-R/L, LOOK is multi-directional, like GIVE. You will learn later the many different meanings which are conveyed by LOOK when the movement and directionality are changed. For the moment, one example will suffice:

"He turned slowly, looked at me, then quickly turned away." MAN IT-R LOOK (Hold hand in R area, fingers pointing towards yourself, then quickly twist the hand back to the original position. This is accompanied by first an anxious facial expression, then a surprised one.)

LOOK
look at, watch, stare

T   V

"Television" must be fingerspelled, T–V. (Fingerspelling is always written in H–Y–P–H–E–N–A–T–E–D capitals.)

TV comes before LOOK, since it is more concrete. Also, you establish a thing that is to be looked at before you look at it.

The "What did you do?" part could be done one of two ways:

1. DO WHAT-SHRUG YOU?

2. YOU?

The second way would be more common, so use it.

Sign: STUDY LITTLE FINISH// TV LOOK-D// YOU?// (The D in LOOK-D means that LOOK ought to be aimed slightly downwards, for that's where the TV set is.)

5. "I visited a deaf friend; we watched a captioned film."

The U.S. Department of Health, Education, and Welfare maintains an agency that leases popular movies, puts sub-titles on them, and distributes them free of charge to deaf groups.

DEAF
deaf

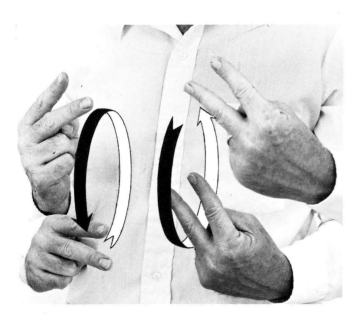

VISIT
visit

HEAR
the sense of hearing; to hear

When HEAR CLOSE are done together, it means "deaf."

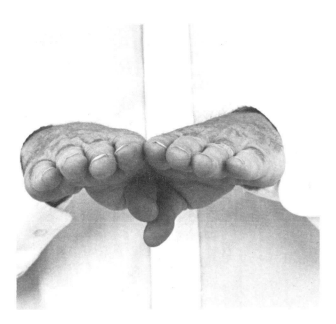

CLOSE
to close, shut

FRIEND
friend

The sign shown in the first set of pictures is the older, original sign. Years ago, some people decided this sign meant, "deaf and dumb," or "deaf mute." Since most deaf people object to being called "dumb" or "mute," the second way of signing it was brought into fashion. It is interesting to note that many deaf people, when they are signing before a group of people, or signing to a hearing person, will generally use HEAR CLOSE, yet when they talk informally among themselves, they use the older DEAF sign.

Further evidence that the DEAF sign has naught to do with dumbness nor muteness is the fact that the movement is just as often from the mouth to the ear as it is from the ear to the mouth. It is stretching the imagination to believe that the signer is thinking, as his hand moves from mouth to ear, "dumb and deaf."

Use whichever sign you feel most comfortable with. Few deaf people will take offense at the older sign.

Some people make this sign by first doing it as shown here, then reversing the position of the hands.

Usually, an adjective follows the sign it modifies, but it may come before. You may sign: FRIEND DEAF, or DEAF FRIEND.

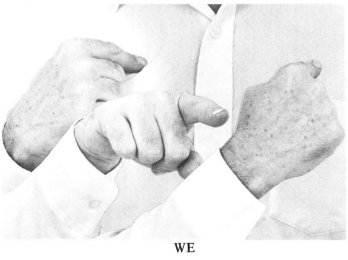

WE
we, us

We may assume there were several people there, so we would sign, WE, not WE-2. However, it would be more common for Ameslan to drop WE altogether.

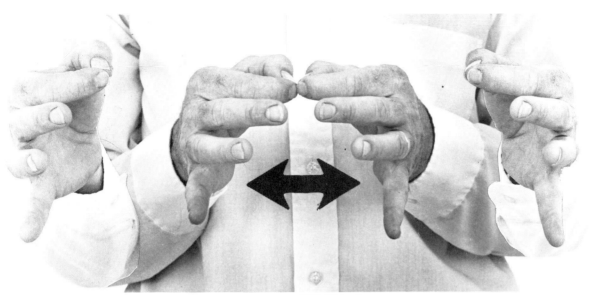

SENTENCE
sentence, statement, line of writing or
print

When SENTENCE is combined with MOVIE, it means, "captioned film," or "a film with sub-titles." Deaf people sometimes refer to these films, or to the groups that meet to see the films, by fingerspelling C—F—D for "captioned film for the deaf."

C

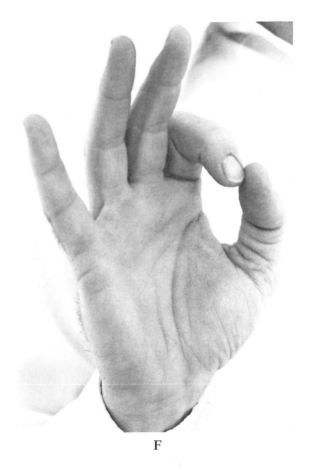

F

6. "Hi! What's up?"

Sign: HELLO//THRILL?//

7. "Nothing. Who's that?" (indicating A)

Use NONE for "nothing," but make it casually. There are three signs for WHO.

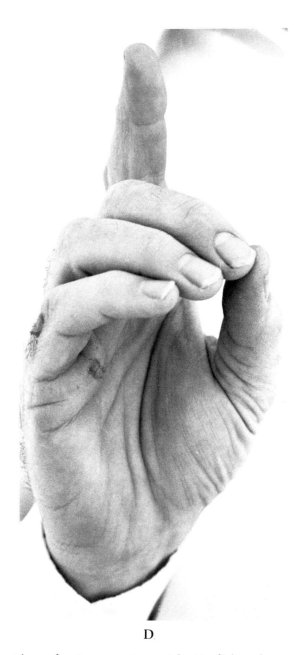

D

When foreign movies with English subtitles are playing at a theatre, deaf people enjoy going to them. They refer to these as, SENTENCE MOVIE. Deaf people also use SENTENCE MOVE to refer to the old silent movies.

Sign: FRIEND DEAF [GO-TO-R] VISIT-R //SENTENCE MOVIE LOOK-U // ("U" means the LOOK Sign should be aimed upwards, for that is where the movie is while it is being watched.)

It is very common to sign GO-TO before VISIT. Notice that GO-TO moves to the R area, and VISIT is done in the R area.

WHO
who, whom, whoever, whomever

60

WHO
· who, whom, whoever, whomever

WHO
who, whom, whoever, whomever

THAT
[1] that, this, it; [2] idiomatically:
"That's it!" "I see," "I understand,"
"So that's it".

When THAT refers to a concrete thing, whether the thing is present or not, make it as shown in the photo. If THAT refers to an abstract thing, as in, "That's a swell idea," it usually is made by slapping the THAT sign into the palm of the other hand. Idiomatically, THAT can mean: "That's it!" (made excitedly, one or both hands), "Ah, yes, I understand," (one hand gently bumped up and down, head nodding).

Often THAT plus indexing are done in sentences such as this one, so you may use either or both.

Sign: NONE//THAT (toward C) IT (toward C) WHO//(WHO THAT (toward C) would be all right too, because there are only two signs involved).

8. "Haven't you two met?"

61

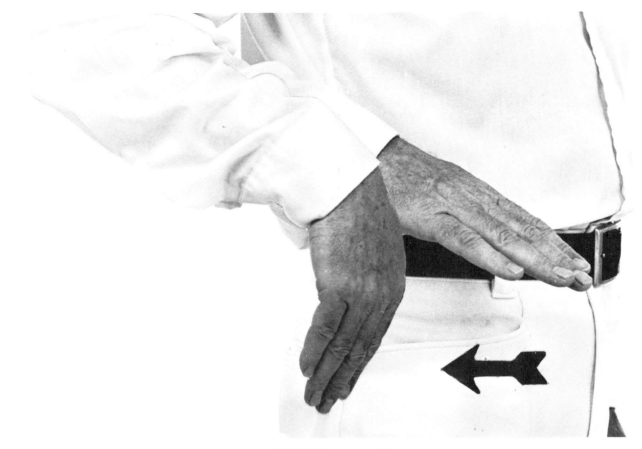

NOT-YET, or LATE
[1] indicates that something has not
yet happened; [2] late, tardy

This sign incorporates two features: [1] negation, and [2] time indication. Because of the negation feature, it follows that which it negates.

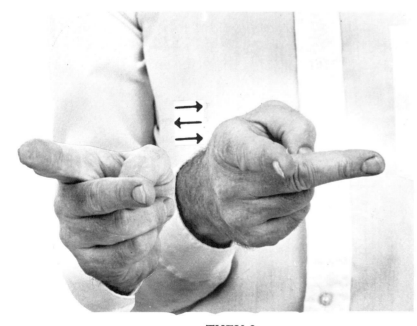

The wrist snaps back and forth, pointing the index finger at one person, then the middle finger at the other person. Repeat it two or three times. You can see that it is a variation of WE-2.

THEY-2.
you two, the two of you, they two,
those two, the two of them

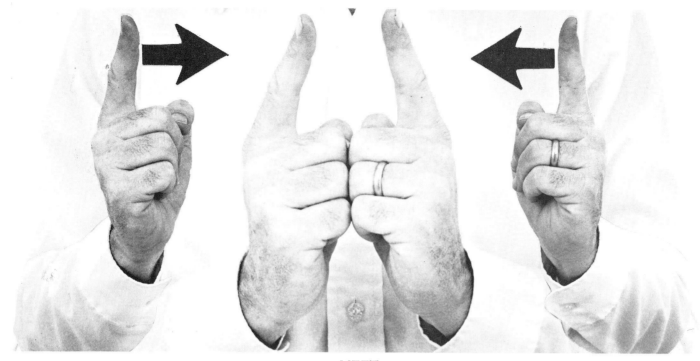

MEET
an encounter between two persons

This sign means only a meeting between two people, not a meeting as in, "Did you go to the committee meeting?"

If you repeat MEET several times, moving it from L to R, it means one person meeting several people.

If you let one hand, say LH, represent yourself by placing it near your chest, and the RH moves from R towards the LH, the meaning is that someone comes up to you. Reversing the action, LH moves to the RH, means you go up to someone.

You may further modify this action by using two fingers on the LH, then move it toward RH in the R area. This means two people went up to one person.

"I go up to someone."

"Someone comes up to me."

THINK
think, thought (verb + noun)

When the hand is moved in a circle near the forehead, it means, "thinking," "wondering," "pondering." The larger the circle becomes, and the more serious the facial expression becomes, the heavier the thinking becomes.

MEET, in this type sentence, is usually done with the RH moving from S to W, and the LH moving from W to S.

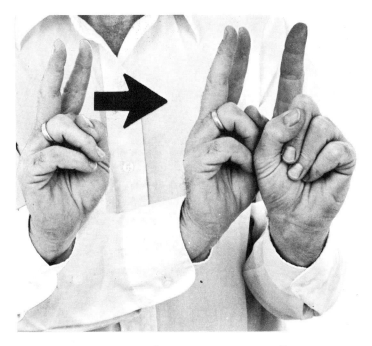

"Two people go up to someone."

"I meet you."

Sign: MEET (LH moves from A, RH moves from C)? NOT-YET ?// You do not need THEY-2, since the LH and RH move from A and C, representing the two of them.

9. "I think I met you once before, but I can't remember."

64

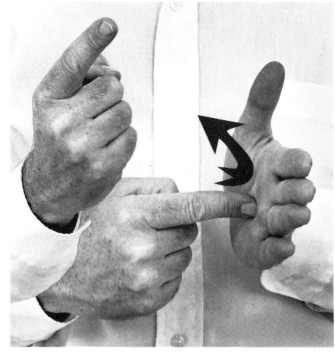

ONCE
one time, once

If the action is repeated, it means, "sometimes." If this same action is repeated slowly, it means, "once in a while," "occasionally." If two fingers are used, it means, "twice," or "double." Three fingers, "thrice," or "triple," or "trebled."

CAN'T
[1] can not, unable, could not; [2] not possible

BUT
[1] but, yet, still, however; [2] different, difference

When BUT is repeated and moved L–R, it means, "many different things."

REMEMBER
remember, recall, recollect

SEEM
seem, appear to be, apparently, could be

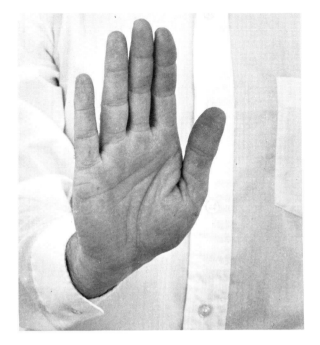

YOUR
your, yours, your own

Sign:

PAST $\begin{smallmatrix}\text{SEEM}\\\text{THINK}\end{smallmatrix}$ MEET (S–W) ONCE $\begin{smallmatrix}\text{THINK}\\\text{SEEM.}\end{smallmatrix}$ // BUT REMEMBER-NEG. CAN'T//

10. "Are you deaf?"

    Sign: DEAF? YOU?//

11. "No, he's/she's hearing. His/her name is Art/Amy, signed ⎯⎯⎯⎯⎯⎯⎯⎯⎯⎯⎯⎯⎯⎯⎯ ."
    (Do name sign)
    " (To A) His/her name is Sam/Sue, signed ⎯⎯⎯⎯⎯⎯⎯⎯⎯⎯⎯⎯⎯⎯⎯ . "
    (Do name sign)

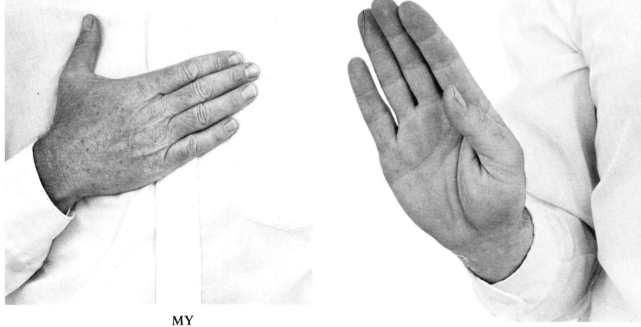

MY
my, mine, my own

ITS
its, his, her, hers

Names of people are fingerspelled, but most deaf people have name-signs, so when introducing a person you may also give the person/s name-sign, though this is not necessary.

If you want to make up a name-sign for yourself, you may. Usually, you take the first letter of your first or last name, and place it on the body somewhere. If a person has a distinguishing physical characteristic, that will often be incorporated into the name-sign.

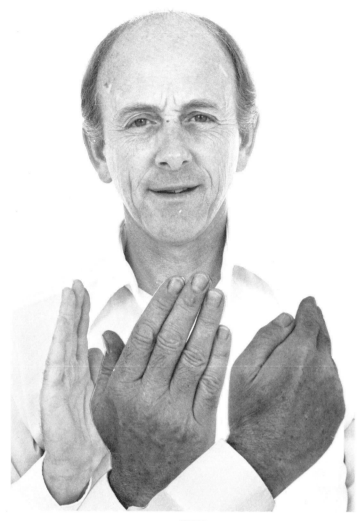

OUR
our, ours, our own

NAME
name, called, label

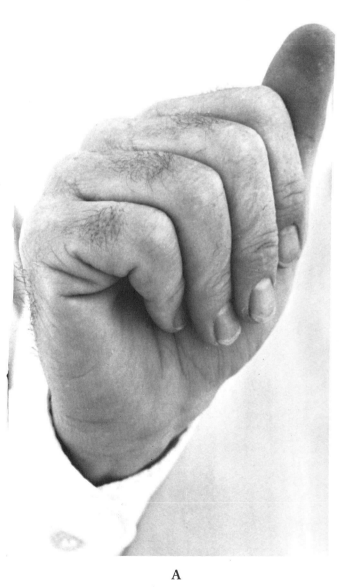

A

67

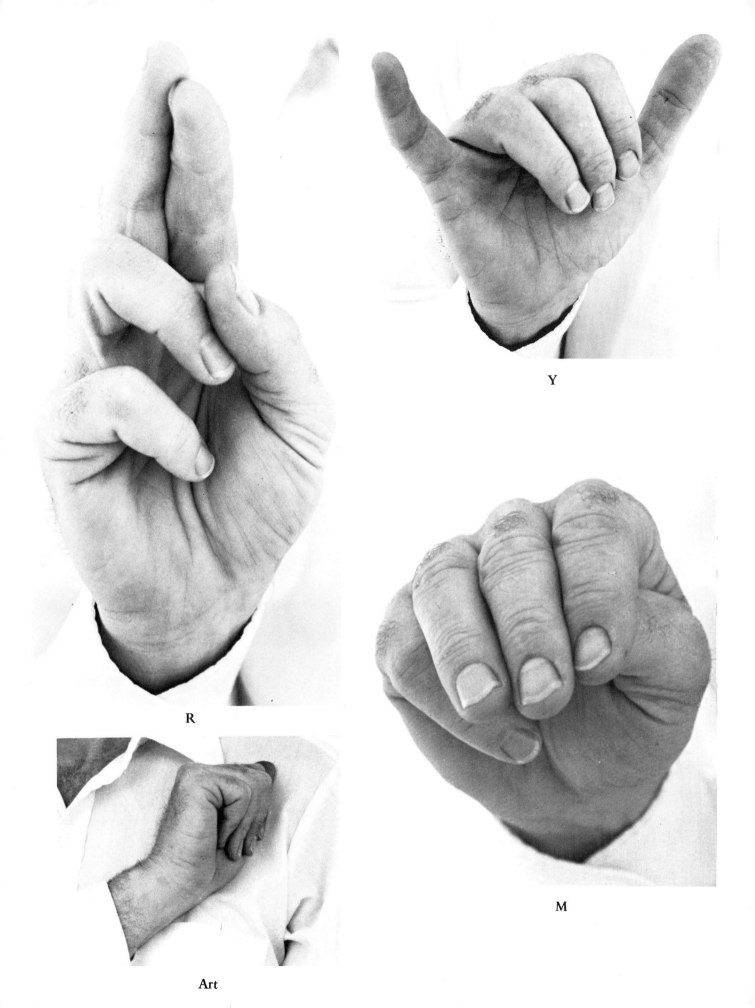

R

Y

M

Art

Amy

Sam

S

U

69

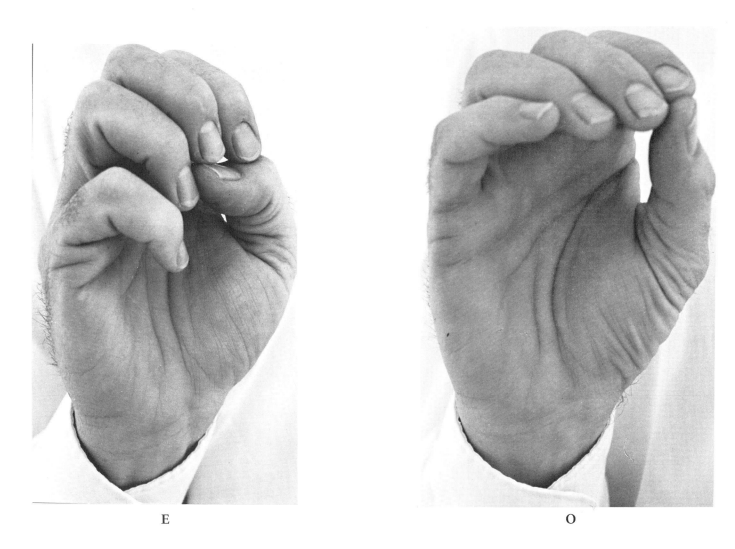

E

O

Sign:

NO//SPEAK//NAME (Towards A) $\begin{matrix} \text{A-R-T} \\ \text{A-M-Y} \end{matrix}$ //SIGN $\begin{matrix} \text{ART} \\ \text{AMY} \end{matrix}$ //NAME (Towards C) $\begin{matrix} \text{S-A-M} \\ \text{S-U-E} \end{matrix}$ //SIGN $\begin{matrix} \text{SAM} \\ \text{SUE} \end{matrix}$ // .

By placing NAME towards or near A and C, you make it clear to whom you are referring, thus the possessive sign, ITS, is not really necessary, so leave it out.

12. (A & C) "Glad to meet you."

Sign:

GLAD MEET (S–W)//

13. "Your name is Bob/Bev, but what's your sign?

Sign:

NAME YOU (TO B) $\begin{matrix} \text{BOB} \\ \text{BEV} \end{matrix}$ //SIGN WHAT-SHRUG //

The YOU is better than YOUR, the idea being, "You are named....."

SUE

70

BUT is often left out. Always use it when contrasting things (You are going, but I am not.), but when no contrast is being made, as in this sentence, then drop the BUT.

Bev

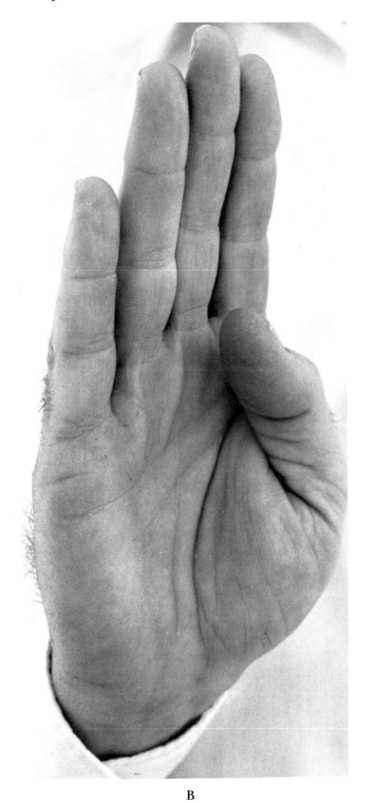

B

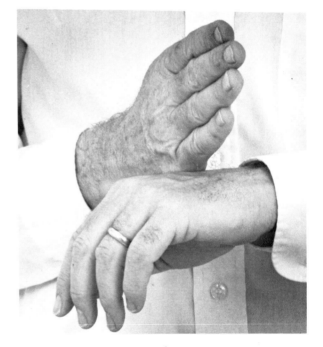

Bob

14. (B shows name-sign.)

15. "Let's go to the snack bar for coffee."

16. (B & C) "All right."

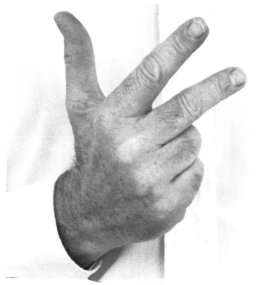

WE-3
we three, the three of us

"Snack bar" is usually fingerspelled: S—B .

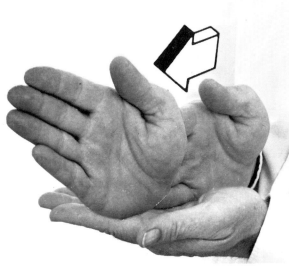

ALLRIGHT
[1] allright, O.K.; [2] right, as in one's right to do something

COFFEE
coffee

Sign: WE- 3 GO-TO-R   S — B//COFFEE//.

FOR is dropped here, as it often is. The facial expression should be partly questioning, and partly saying, "Yes, let's go."

K

72

Sign: ALLRIGHT // or O–K //

ADDITIONAL VOCABULARY

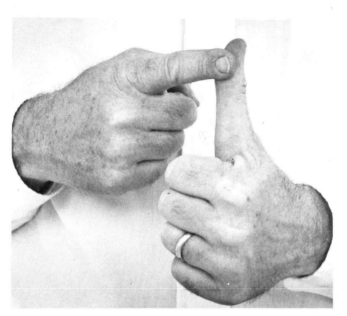

FIRST
first

LAST
last or final in a series

When giving your name, you may simply finger-spell it, but often deaf people will first sign: FIRST, then fingerspell their first name; next, sign LAST, then fingerspell their last name. Sometimes they will reverse the order giving their last name first, so be prepared for it.

ALLRIGHT	NOT-YET
AMY	ONCE
AND	ONLY
ART	ONLY-ONE
BEV	OUR
BOB	PRACTICE
BUT	REMEMBER
CAN'T	SAM
CLOSE	SEEM
COFFEE	SENTENCE
DEAF	SIGN
DO	SPEAK
FIRST	STUDY
FRIEND	SUE
HEAR	THAT
ITS	THEY-2
LAST	THINK
LET	VISIT
LITTLE	WE
LOOK	WE-2
MEET	WE-3
MY	WHAT
NAME	WHAT-SHRUG
NO	WHO
NONE	YOUR

"I go up to someone."
"Someone comes up to me."
"Two people go up to someone."
"I meet you."

Fingerspelling: A B C D E F K M O

R S T U V Y

EXERCISE 17

Translate and practice

1. A friend came over to visit last night. I hadn't seen him in a long time. ("in a long time"—UP-TILL-NOW)

2. I don't understand this sentence.

3. Haven't you done your work yet?

4. You're late, he's already gone.

5. When you're done studying, we'll go have coffee.

6. You seem happy, what happened? Yesterday you felt lousy.

7. I have to meet a man, so I think I'll go now. (Ameslan has no "so.")

8. Someone told me you are sick.

9. You're the only one I love.

10. I'll do it myself!

11. You helped me a little, but she helped me most.

12. What's he saying?

13. What are you looking at me for?

14. All right, I'll let you go, but you must come back here tomorrow.

15. I went to several places, but they all said, "No."

16. I've seen that movie before.

17. I saw him give you something.

18. Who told you I overslept?

19. I can't study, I'm too excited! (Intensification of the THRILL sign will convey the idea of "very excitedly," "too excited!"

20. You're supposed to do it yourself.

DIALOGUE (A, B, AND C ARE IN THE SNACK BAR)

Memorize and practice with two other people.

A: I like my coffee black.
B: I've tried to drink it black, but I don't like it.
C: You have to keep trying.
B: I have, but I just can't get used to it. I've got to have cream and sugar.
C: I prefer tea with lemon.
A: (To C) Are you married?
C: Yes, my husband/wife is a student.
B: What's he/she studying?
C: Science, he/she wants to be a doctor.
A: My father's a doctor, but I want to be a teacher.
B: (To C) Do you have any children?
C: No, we'll wait a few years.
B: My mother's a teacher, what do you want to be?
C: I don't know, I haven't decided yet.
A: Looks as if it might snow.
B: I don't think so, looks like rain to me.
C: Well, ready to go, or do you want to stay?
A: It doesn't matter to me.
B: I've got to go before it rains.
C: I think I'll stay for a while.

B: See you later.
A&C: Goodbye.

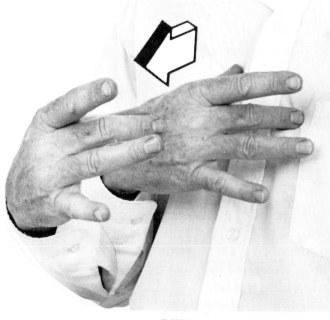

LIKE
[1] like, be attracted to; [2] interested in, interesting

INTERESTING
[1] interesting, be interested in, be
absorbed with; [2] look at, observe
watch

EXPLANATION

1. "I like my coffee black."

Often LIKE is made with both hands, which intensifies the meaning. INTERESTING is not used for "like," "enjoy," etc.. LIKE is not used for "observing," "looking at," etc..

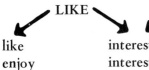

LIKE		INTERESTING
like	interesting	observing
enjoy	interested in	looking at
prefer	absorbing	watching intently

Sign: **LIKE COFFEE BLACK ME//**

My is omitted. The meaning is: "I like black coffee." Ameslan thinks of liking black coffee, rather than possessing it. LIKE expresses an emotional reaction, hence it often follows that to which it refers: COFFEE BLACK//LIKE ME//.

BLACK
black

2. "I've tried to drink it black, but I don't like it."

Sign: TRY BLACK (TRY) BUT//DON'T-LIKE//

DRINK is omitted since it is understood from the context.

TRY is often copied.

Naturally, "it" is omitted because it is obvious what you are talking about.

DRINK
to drink any non-alcoholic beverage

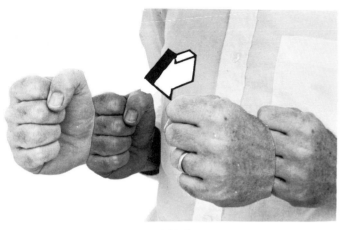

TRY
try, attempt, strive

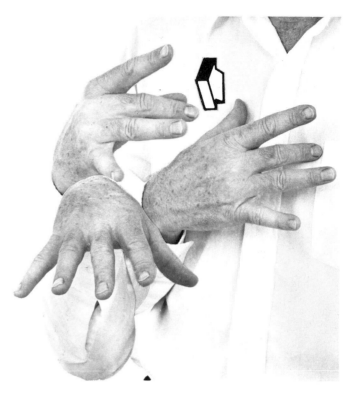

DON'T-LIKE
do not like, not attracted to

COCKTAIL
Usually an alcoholic drink such as a
cocktail.

DRUNK

BOOZE
usually refers to alcoholic drinks, or drinking
and has a humorous or strongly negative
feeling to it.

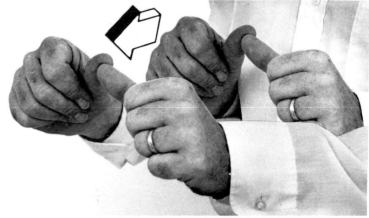

CONTINUE
to keep at a task, continue, stay with it, keep on

3. "You have to keep trying."

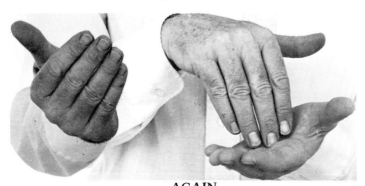

AGAIN
again, repeat, over, once more

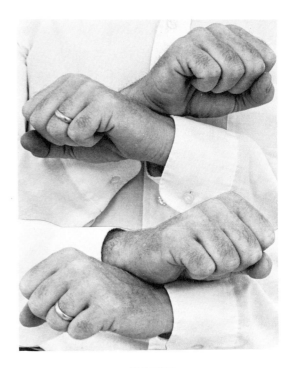

HABIT
[1] habit; [2] custom, tradition; [3] to
become used to, get accustomed to

OFTEN
often, frequently

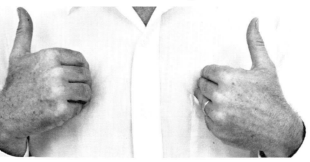

HAVE
[1] to possess, have, own; [2] sometimes means "there are," "there were,"
etc.

If AGAIN is repeated, it could be used in
this sentence: AGAIN-3 MUST, meaning,
"You have to do it over and over again."
When AGAIN is repeated, its meaning is
not the same as OFTEN.

Sign: [MUST] TRY//CONTINUE MUST//.

BOX
any cubical object, box, room.

If MUST is copied, it means S is making a
very emphatic statement.

When you make a sign using the first letter of the
English word, it is called an initialized sign. The
BOX sign with an "O" would mean "office."
Many initialized signs are used in schools for deaf
children, and some of them are too now to have
become widespread in the general population, so
exercise care in using them.

4. "I have, but I just can't get used to it. I've got
to have cream and sugar."

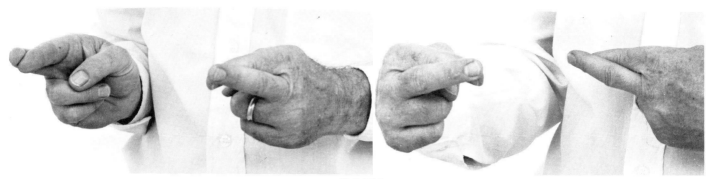

ROOM
the initialized sign for room

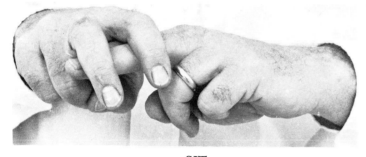

SIT
(1) sit, sit down, have a seat; (2) chair, seat stool, bench.

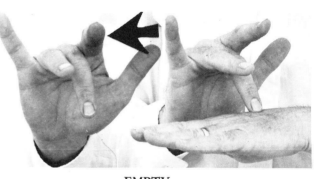

EMPTY
(1) blank, empty, vacant; (2) naked, bare. "There are no chairs in that empty room."

Sign: ROOM INX-R EMPTY//SIT HAVE NONE//

The phrase, "I've got to have" may be signed, HAVE MUST, but another way to sign it would be to use:

If you wish to sign "Are there any books?" sign: BOOK HAVE?//. For "There is paper over there," sign: PAPER HAVE INDEX R//.

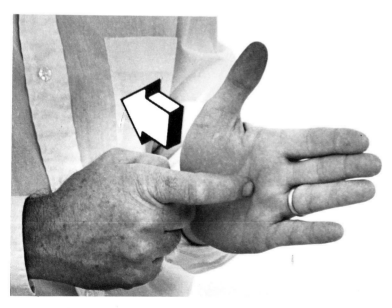

REQUIRE
[1] require, demand, insist upon, got to have;   [2] qualifications for a job or certificate

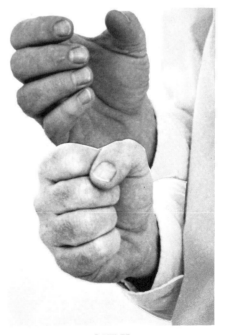

MILK
milk (verb + noun)

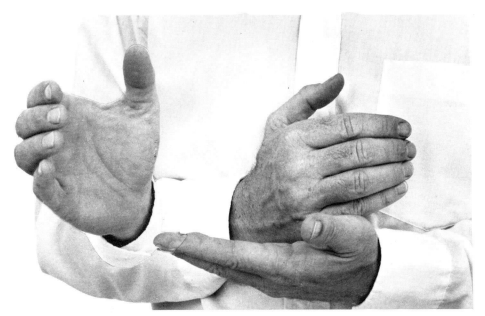

CREAM, or EARN
[1] cream; [2] skim off the top;
[3] earn money

When CREAM is made larger and bumpy, it means
to collect.

SUGAR, or SWEET
[1] sugar, sweet, candy; [2] candy

Often this sign will be made with only two
fingers. The sign for "candy" varies widely
from state to state.

Sign: FINISH//BUT HABIT CAN'T//
CREAM SUGAR REQUIRE//. One of the
uses of FINISH is to express the idea, "I
did!", "I have!", meaning that whatever is
being discussed is a past event. In this case,
the thing being discussed is, "Try to drink
black coffee." The answer: "I have tried
it!"

Remember that the negative, CAN'T, follows that which it negates.

You could substitute MUST for REQUIRE,
or use both: REQUIRE CREAM SUGAR
MUST. It would be unusual to use HAVE
here, since you are not possessing the
cream and sugar.

5. "I prefer tea with lemon."

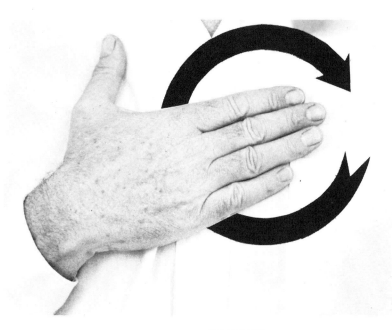

PLEASE
[1] please as in, "Please don't do that!"
[2] pleasing, pleasure, enjoy, like

This sign may be used to answer a question such as, "Would you like some coffee?" or to make a request, "Please don't eat the daisies."

In expressing pleasure and enjoyment, it conveys a stronger feeling than LIKE. "Liking" a thing is not quite the same as "enjoying" it.

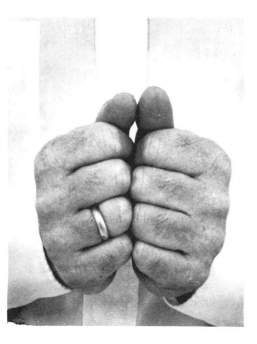

WITH
with, together, side by side

WITH is used primarily to locate an object. It is rarely used in such sentences as, "She was filled with terror," "He looked with a determined eye," and "With what you know, you ought to be able to get a job." These uses of "with" do not locate concrete objects. In general, prepositions relate to the physical positions of the items being discussed.

When WITH is moved, say L—R, it means, "to go with," "to go together," "to accompany."

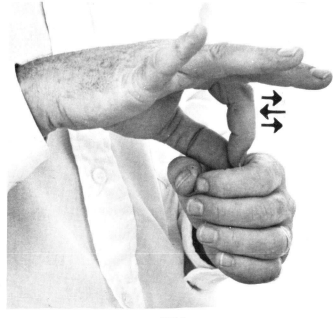

TEA
tea

SOUR
sour; pickle

The sign for "lemon" is made differently in different parts of the country, so you must check with local deaf people as to how they sign it. The "sour" meaning here would imply "lemon" because of the context. In a different context, of course, the sign might mean "pickle."

6. (To C) "Are you married?"

MARRY
to get married, to be married

Sign: MARRY? YOU?//.

7. "Yes. My husband/wife is a student."

BITTER, or MISS
[1] bitter; [2] disappoint; [3] miss, yearn, long for

LIKE BETTER

Sign: TEA WITH SOUR//
        PLEASE

S could sign, PLEASE (Plus COMPARA-TIVE MARKER) for "prefer," but it would be more common to sign just, PLEASE. You may copy, LIKE BETTER, or PLEASE.

HUSBAND
[1] husband; [2] believe

82

BELIEVE
believe

The reason HUSBAND may also mean "believe" is due to the way the two signs have evolved. Originally, "husband" was signed, MAN MARRY. Eventually the MAN sign was dropped, and often the THINK is dropped. You may often see BELIEVE signed THINK MARRY, but it is very rare to see HUSBAND signed MAN MARRY.

WIFE
wife

Originally WIFE was, GIRL MARRY.

Originally, "woman" was GIRL plus an indication of a tall person, while "girl" was GIRL plus an indication of a short person. This is still done to some extent today. The same was done to distinguish between "man" and "boy."

The sign WOMAN is also the blending of two signs. First, GIRL was signed, then RH moved to the chest, making the sign from which FINE eventually evolved. Today, you may still see "woman" signed GIRL FINE.

While we are still in a historical vein, the sign for "gentleman" is,

AGENT, or PERSON
[1] a marker that denotes the person who does the thing signified by the sign immediately ahead of it; [2] person, individual

So, "student" is STUDY AGENT. But a more common way to sign "student" is,

GENTLEMAN
gentleman, gentlemen

It evolved from MAN FINE. It is used almost exclusively to open a speech, "Ladies and gentlemen...."

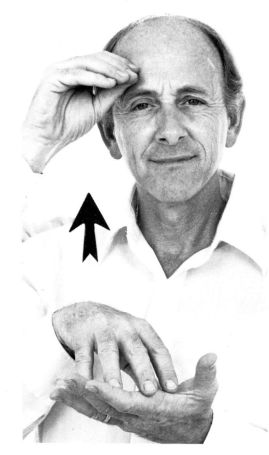

LEARN
learn

84

Thus, "student" is LEARN AGENT.

How would you sign: giver, helper, a home body, observer, lover, speaker, visitor, and worker?

Sometimes the AGENT sign is made in front of S, or to R/L of S.

Sign: YES//MY HUSBAND/WIFE LEARN AGENT//.

PERSON
the AGENT sign initialized with "P's"

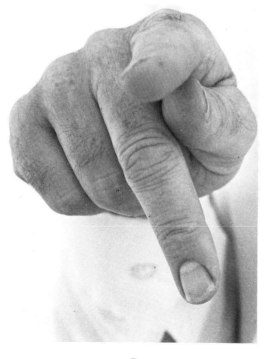

P

8.   "What's he/she studying?"

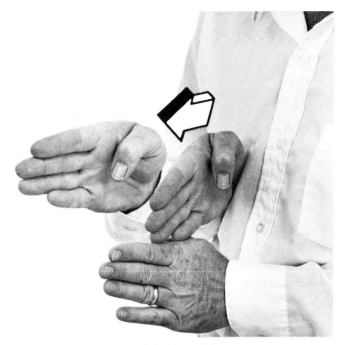

STRAIGHT
[1] straight; [2] career, profession, line of work; [3] academic major field of study

This sign is often used when asking a deaf person what kind of work they do, e.g., WORK STRAIGHT WHAT-SHRUG// and sometimes even the WORK is dropped. In schools it is used to designate one's major subject of study. So, when asking a student what he is studying, use the STRAIGHT sign.

Sign: (HUSBAND/WIFE) STRAIGHT WHAT-SHRUG//.

The "he/she" of English is unnecessary in Ameslan here, for the context of the whole conversation makes it clear about whom B is inquiring. However, it would not be wrong to sign HUSBAND/WIFE here if you wish. YOUR is usually dropped when the context is as explicit as this one is.

9. "Science, he/she wants to be a doctor."

SCIENCE
science

"Chemistry" is often initialized with C's, and "biology" with B's.

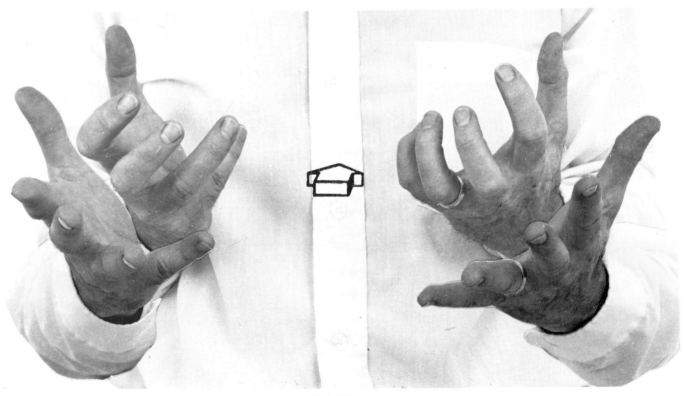

WANT
want, desire, wish, yearn

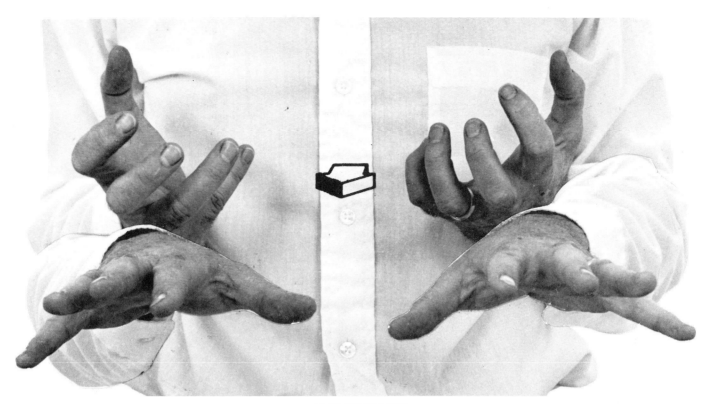

DON'T–WANT
do not want

This is another of those signs where an alteration of the sign negates the meaning.

GOAL
[1] goal, objective; [2] aim, purpose

This sign covers the whole phrase, "wants to be."

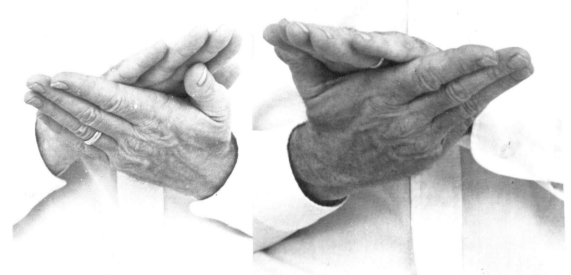

BECOME
become, be, turn into, take on some
quality

English expressions such as, "He took ill,"
require BECOME, e.g., INDEX R/L BE-
COME SICK//. "The frog turned into a
prince," requires BECOME for "turned
into."

DOCTOR
doctor, physician

Often DOCTOR is initialized with a D.

Sign: SCIENCE//GOAL (BECOME) DOC-
TOR//.

"10. My father's a doctor, but I want to be a teacher."

TEACH
teach, instruct

Sign: MY FATHER DOCTOR//BUT ME
GOAL (BECOME) TEACH (AGENT)//.
The AGENT sign is optional. It is often
left off, and you may think, "I want to
teach," rather than, "I want to be a teacher."

11. (To C) "Do you have any children?"

CHILDREN
children

To sign "child," make one movement downward, do not repeat the sign moving to the side. Often this sign will be preceded by BOY or GIRL, to indicate the sex of the child.

Sign: CHILDREN? HAVĖ? (ANY?)//.

12. "No, we'll wait a few years."

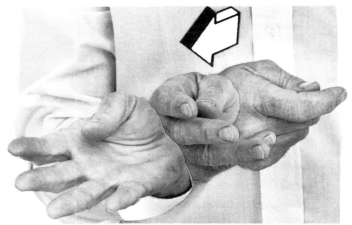

FEW, or SEVERAL
few, not many, several

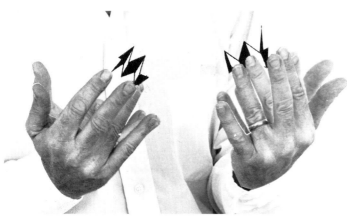

WAIT
wait, wait for

When "few" is meant, make the sign smaller; when "several" is meant, make it larger. FEW sometimes follows that to which it refers, as do most quantifiers including numbers.

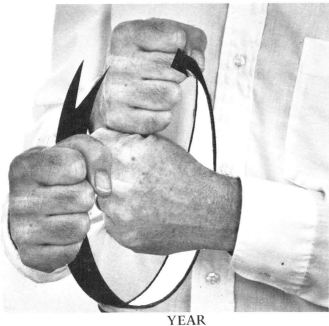

YEAR
year

DON'T-KNOW
do not know

Sign: NO
NONE   //WAIT FEW YEAR//
NOT-YET

Any one of the three negative signs works here. NO answers the question in the negative; NONE says, "We don't have any;" NOT YET says, "We don't have any yet."

WAIT may be copied.

13. "My mother's a teacher. What do you want to be?"

Sign: MY MOTHER TEACH//YOU GOAL WHAT-SHRUG YOU//.

Be sure there is a pause between the two sentences.

14. "I don't know, I haven't decided yet."

KNOW
know, knowledge

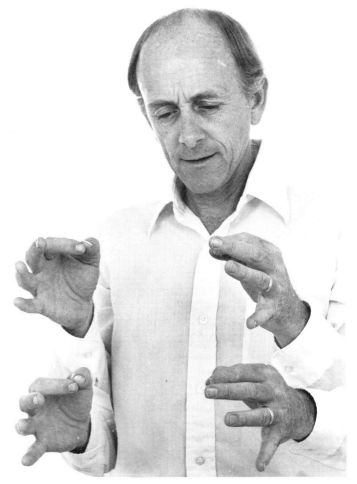

DECIDE
[1] reach a decision, decide, conclude;
[2] decisive, definite; [3] steadfast, firm
in resolve

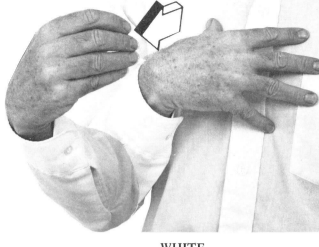

WHITE
white

JUDGE
[1] to judge, referee, weigh a matter;
[2] court, trial; [3] if (usually only in
poems and songs)

Sign: DON'T-KNOW //DECIDE NOT-YET//.

15. "Looks as if it might snow."

SNOW
snow

MAYBE
maybe, perhaps, possibly, might

Usually, "snow" is signed, WHITE SNOW,
using BH for WHITE.

Sign: SEEM WHITE SNOW SEEM// or,
MAYBE WHITE SNOW MAYBE//, or,
SEEM WHITE SNOW MAYBE//.

SEEM may mean, "looks as if."

16. "I don't think so, looks like rain to me."

DOUBT
to be uncertain about something, doubt

NOT
a negative used primarily for denial;
not, do not, does not, did not, is not
are not, were not

To sign, "I don't think so" as, THINK-NEG. NOT, is possible, but because NOT is used primarily to deny a fact, it is better to sign DISBELIEVE.

DISBELIEVE expresses S's certainty that something is not true.

DOUBT, on the other hand, expresses S's uncertainty that something is true.

The critical difference hinges upon what S is sure of. If S is sure that a thing is not true, S signs DISBELIEVE. If S is not sure that a thing is true, S signs DOUBT.

DISBELIEVE: sure a thing is not true, not so, will not or did not happen.

DOUBT: not sure a thing is true, is so, will or did happen.

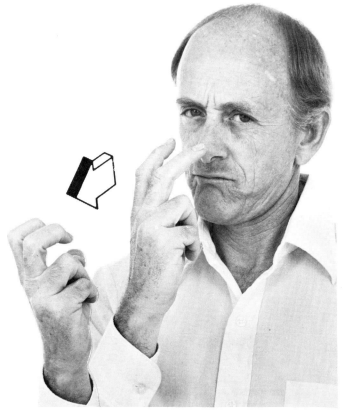

DISBELIEVE
not to believe that something is so

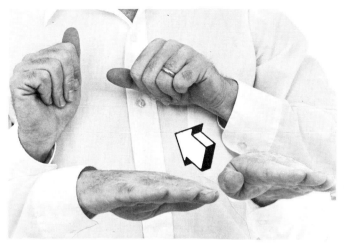

RAIN
rain

DEPART
depart, leave

By now you certainly are aware of Ameslan's characteristic dropping of subject pronouns. Here is a good example. Ameslan rarely puts in the "I," as in, "I don't think so." And it has no use for the, "to me," at the end of this sentence. To deaf people, these pronouns are understood, and signed only when S wishes to emphasize them.

Often you have a choice of using DEPART, or GO, since they are similar in meaning. DEPART is used mostly when S wishes to sign that he left some place which S has already spatialized R/L, i.e., DEPART-R-S, or DEPART-L-S.

17. "Well, ready to go, or do you want to stay?"

READY
ready

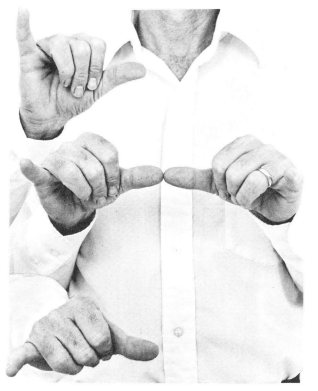

STAY
stay, remain

Often STAY is done with one hand, which makes it look identical to THAT done with one hand. Context dictates which sign is intended.

STAY is directional in that you may STAY R/L/U as well as D.

WHICH
[1] which; [2] whether; [3] or

When you make a statement that involves a choice between two or more things, use WHICH: "Do you want coffee or tea?" WANT COFFEE//(WHICH) TEA//WHICH?//. Since WHICH is used here as an interrogative, it comes last.

When you list several things in a series, use WHICH to mean, "or:" "Whether there be floods, or famines, or fires, or earthquakes, we shall endure," the "or's" are signed WHICH.

A sentence such as, "It may rain, or it may snow, I don't know," could be signed, MAYBE RAIN (WHICH) MAYBE SNOW// WHICH?// DON'T-KNOW //. The first WHICH is used as, "or," and is optional. The second WHICH is used as an interrogative. It is a common practice in Ameslan to ask a question that requires no answer. This is called the rhetorical question device. The S often asks the question, then answers it himself. This will be discussed more thoroughly in Lesson 14.

Never use WHICH in a sentence such as, "You may not go, which is what I told you yesterday." There is no choice between alternatives being expressed here, there is no "or" idea, and there is no question being asked, so WHICH is not used.

Sign: SHRUG GO-R/L DEPART READY?//STAY WANT//WHICH?//

18. "It doesn't matter to me."

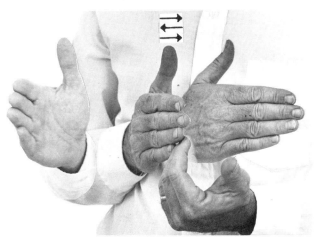

NO-MATTER
[1] it does not matter, makes no difference; [2] nevertheless, regardless, in spite of

DON'T-CARE
do not care

NO-MATTER is often used for, "don't care," the idea being that if it does not matter to me, then I do not care.

Sign: NO-MATTER
                          //
        DON'T-CARE

19. "I've got to go before it rains."

BEFORE
before, preceding, previous, prior, former

Sign:

GO-R/L
                        MUST BEFORE RAIN//
DEPART

20. "I think I'll stay for a while."

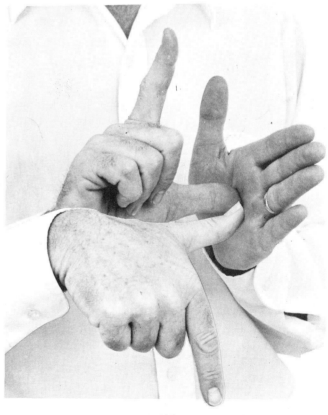

LATER
[1] later, later on; [2] awhile

LATER means for a time into the future. Do not confuse it with the English comparative form of "late." "I'll see you later," vs. "You are later than he." The comparative form is signed, NOT-YET COMP.

95

When LATER means "awhile," it is done slowly, as opposed to doing it faster when it means, "later."

Sign: (THINK) STAY LATER//.

21. "See you later."

When signing LATER, the LH is often not used. Practice combining SEE LATER smoothly without using LH.

22. "Goodbye."

Sign: HELLO
GOODBYE//
SELF

NEW SIGNS TO REVIEW:

AGAIN	KNOW
AGENT	LATER
ANY	LEARN
BECOME	LIKE
BEFORE	MAYBE
BELIEVE	MAJOR
BITTER	MARRY
BLACK	MILK
BOOZE	NO-MATTER
BOX	NOT
CHILDREN	OFTEN
COCKTAIL	PERSON
CONTINUE	PLEASE
CREAM	RAIN
DECIDE	READY
DEPART	REQUIRE
DISBELIEVE	ROOM
DOCTOR	SCIENCE
DON'T-CARE	SIT
DON'T-KNOW	SNOW
DON'T-LIKE	SOUR
DON'T-WANT	STAY
DOUBT	STRAIGHT
DRINK	SUGAR
EMPTY	TEA
FEW	TEACH
GENTLEMAN	TRY
GOAL	WAIT
HABIT	WANT
HAVE	WHICH
HUSBAND	WHITE
INTERESTING	WIFE
JUDGE	WITH
	YEAR

FINGERSPELLING

EXERCISE 18

Translate and practice.

1. You remember Art? A few days ago he went to visit his parents, but they were not at home.

2. It doesn't matter whether you believe it or not.

3. After they are married, they want to be teachers of deaf children.

4. How did the doctor know you were sick? I didn't tell him.

5. I'm not used to studying yet.

6. That's not what I told you!

7. I don't care if you are sick, get out of here and go to work, right now!

8. You must try; it takes practice.

9. What do you want?

10. For a long time now, I've wanted to give you something.

11. Please wait out there, someone will be there later.

12. I doubt if the room is empty.

13. Are you happy you decided to stay here?

14. We went to a movie last night, but it was closed, so we went home.

15. That woman gave me something interesting. Do you want to see it?

16. I know you don't want to go, but you really ought to.

17. All right, you can go with me just this once, that's all.

18. You've got several books.

19. That's the girl who told me.

20. I didn't know you liked coffee.

21. Please understand, I tried to help her, but she didn't want it.

22. Don't you believe me?

23. Please sit down, open your books, and study.

24. It's allright for you to go, but get back here before sundown.

25. He drank a little bit, then he got sick.

26. You should do the work yourself; he can't do it.

27. I can't decide which book I want.

28. She wants to be a scientist.

29. I'll miss you when you've gone.

30. Have you decided whether you want to practice or study?

NOTES

Reporting what was said by people who are not present can become quite complicated in Ameslan. If, for example, S wishes to relate to W a conversation S had with someone, S will use a good deal of role playing. Suppose the following conversation is what S wishes to relate to W:

Yesterday, I met my friend.
"How are you?" I said.
"Fine, how are you?" she said.
"Where are you going?" I asked.
"Home. See you later," she said.
I said, "Fine! Take care!"
Then I went home.

S may simply sign: YESTERDAY MEET-R FRIEND-R //ME SPEAK//HOW IT-R?//IT-R SPEAK//FINE//YOU?// and so on. It is more likely, however, that S will combine with these signs something called body shifting (BS). The BS is a slight twisting of the upper torso toward the right (BSR), left (BSL). When the body returns to the front, the normal face to face position with S and W, it is called body shift to the front (BSF).

So, S would most likely sign in the following way:

YESTERDAY MEET-R   FRIEND-R //ME

At this point, S twists slightly to the right while signing, SPEAK//

(BSR) HOW YOU?//

S signs YOU, not IT-R, because S and friend are now in the normal S-W position. Then S twists while at the same time signing, IT-R SPEAK// and signs:

(BSL) FINE//YOU?//

WHERE
where, whence

GOING
go, with emphasis on the act of going
itself

This sign differs from GO and GO-TO only in emphasis. Whereas, GO emphasizes going from a place, and GO-TO stresses going to a place, GOING accentuates the act of going itself. It is the sign to use, for example, in the question, "Where are we going?"

in such sentences as, "Do you want to go?" QUERY//GO-TO R? WANT? YOU?//. In this sentence, QUERY is not usually copied.

QUERY
[1] to ask a question, to inquire;
[2] idiomatically: "Do you?" "Did
you?"

QUERY
[1] to ask a question, to inquire;
[2] idiomatically: "Do you?" "Did
you?"

An idiomatic use of QUERY which expresses a feeling of skepticism, or doubt, occurs in such sentences as: "Do you really think he's sick?" QUERY//IT-R? SICK? (TRUE?) QUERY//. And

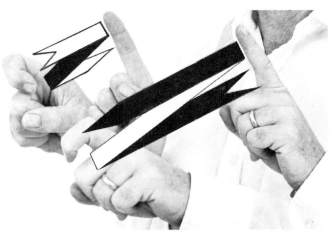

INTERROGATE
to ask a lot of questions, to interrogate,
to interview (verb + noun)

Now S shifts R, while signing, QUERY-R//. The signing of SPEAK//, QUERY//, or TELL//, while simultaneously twisting the body from R-L, or from L-R, seems to tie things together neatly, leaving no "dead" space.

(BSR) GOING WHERE//

SPEAK//

(BSL) HOME//SEE LATER//

TELL-R//

(BSR) FINE//SELF!//

Now S returns from the past to the present by resuming the normal S-W position.

(BSF) ME GO-R HOME//

In addition to the BS, S shows by facial expression the different feelings expressed by S and the friend.

ADDITIONAL VOCABULARY

QUESTIONNAIRE
a list of questions, questionnaire, an
application, a test, an examination

LONG-AGO
[1] sometime in the past, usually at
least several years ago; [2] express
past habitual action, "...used to..."

TEST
test, exam, quiz

SCHOOL
school

NEW SIGNS TO REVIEW

GOING
INTERROGATE
LONG-AGO
QUERY
QUESTIONNAIRE
SCHOOL
TEST
WHERE

EXERCISE 19

Translate and practice.

Once, long ago, Art and Sam were on their way to school.

Art said, "I don't want to go to school, do you?"

"No," Sam said, "let's do something different!"

"Let's go to a movie," Art said.

Sam asked, "Do you think it's allright?"

"Sure!" said Art.

"Okay, let's go!" Sam said.

So the two of them didn't go to school, they went to a movie.

LESSON **13**

Once upon a time, a hare was bragging about how fast he could run. He challenged the other animals to race him. A lowly tortoise accepted the challenge.

"You! You think you can beat me?" exclaimed the hare.

"Yep," replied the tortoise.

"Very well. Are you ready?" asked the hare.

"Ready," replied the tortoise.

"Fox, will you be the starter?" the hare asked.

The fox stepped up and said, "On your marks, set, go!"

The hare took off in a cloud of dust, while the tortoise lumbered slowly behind. After awhile, the hare stopped, and sat down to rest, knowing the tortoise to be hopelessly behind. The warm sun made the hare drowsy, and he fell into a deep sleep.

By and by, the tortoise shuffled up. He gave the sleeping hare a glance, and trudged on toward the finish line.

About a half-hour later, a fly lit on the hare's nose and awakened him. The hare leaped to his feet, and dashed for the finish line. Just as the hare reached the finish line, he saw the tortoise sitting on the other side, smiling.

"You tricked me!" screamed the hare, "I'm faster than you are, and you know it!"

"Mebbe so," drawled the tortoise, "but speed up 'n' stop won't never beat slow 'n' steady."

TRANSLATION

1. "Once upon a time, a hare was bragging about how fast he could run."

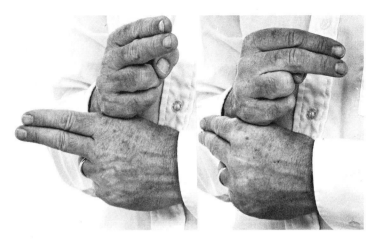

RABBIT
rabbit, hare

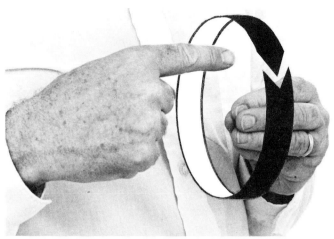

ABOUT
[1] about, regarding, with reference
to; [2] approximately

RABBIT
rabbit, hare

RAPID
rapid, very quick, very fast

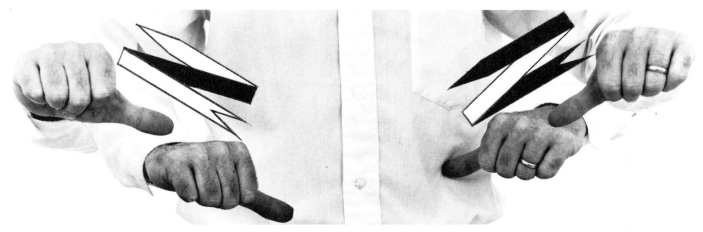

BRAG
brag, boast

RUN
usually means to run a foot race

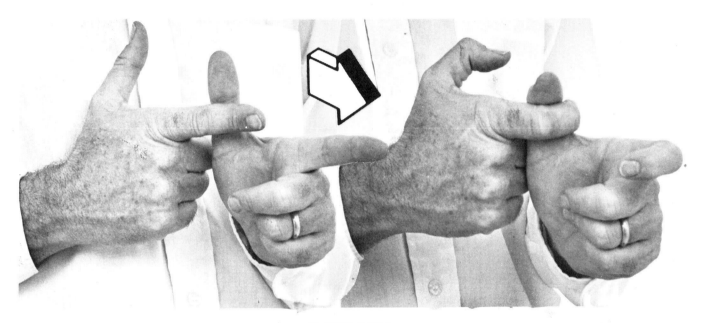

RAPID-RUN
to run very fast

Both RUN and RAPID-RUN move in all directions except toward S.

"Once upon a time," is usually signed, ONCE LONG-AGO.

Although there is no indication in English of what the hare actually said, Ameslan shows it is the rabbit talking by indexing, then by facial expression and character signing show it is the rabbit saying, "I run really fast."

Sign: ONCE LONG-AGO//RABBIT IT-R BRAG//ME RAPID-RUN ME//BRAG IT-R.

2. "He challenged the other animals to race him."

OTHER
[1] other, another; [2] else

CHALLENGE
[1] challenge, dare; [2] game, match,
contest

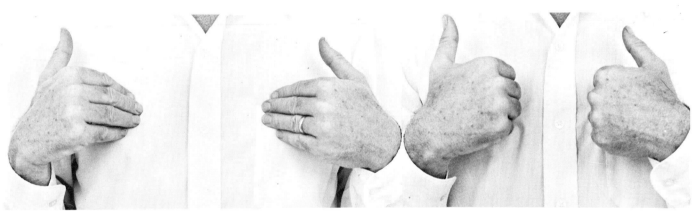

ANIMAL
animal, creature

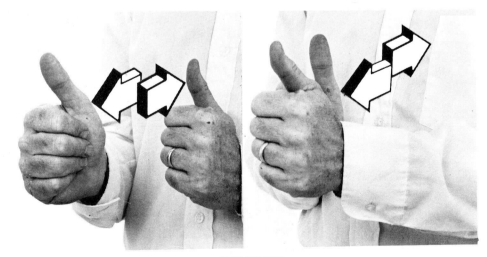

COMPETE
competition, compete, contest

Sign: IT-R CHALLENGE OTHER ANIMAL//COMPETE CHALLENGE//.

Another, more interesting way to sign this would be to continue playing the role of the hare. Instead of dropping the rabbit character and signing, BRAG IT-R// continue the rabbit character and sign: CHALLENGE ANIMAL// "gesture to the 'animals' "//COMPETE? WANT?//

The meaning is, "I challenge any of you animals to race me, anyone willing?"

As S signs COMPETE? WANT?// look L—R smiling slyly. This reinforces the egotism of the rabbit character.

3. "A lowly tortoise accepted the challenge."

TURTLE
turtle, tortoise, terrapin

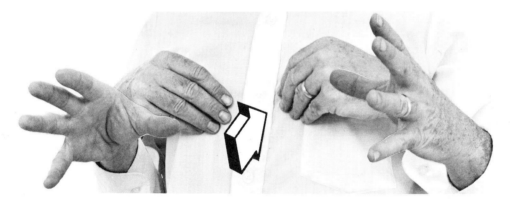

ACCEPT
[1] accept; [2] comply with, acceed,
conform to, resign oneself to

HAPPEN
[1] happen, take place, occur;
[2] event, happening; [3] accident

107

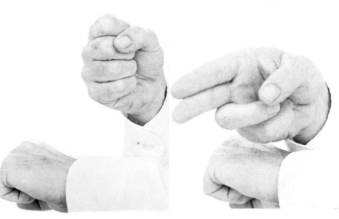

CAN often follows the thing to which it refers. In this sentence, it follows BEAT.

BEAT
beat, defeat, conquer, overcome

HUMBLE
humble, modest, humility

Often HAPPEN is used to introduce a topic, or some new facet of a topic.

Sign: (Do not forget to step out of the rabbit character back into your role as narrator.)

HAPPEN TURTLE IT-LD//ACCEPT CHALLENGE//ACCEPT//.

Think of HAPPEN here as, "Now there happened to be..." or, "By chance there was a ..."

4. " 'You! You think you can beat me?' exclaimed the hare."

BEAT
beat, defeat, conquer, overcome

 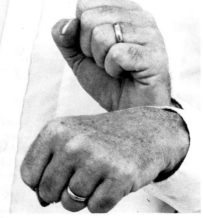

CAN
[1] can, able, could; [2] possible

Both BEAT signs are multi-directional.

Sign: (BSL) YOU!//THINK BEAT W—S?
CAN?//YOU?//

When the hare is addressing the tortoise, S bends forward slightly, and signs downward to show the difference in height between the two. This helps make the picture clearer.

5. " 'Yep,' replied the tortoise."

COMMAND
to give an order, issue a command,
dictate, prescribe

ANSWER
[1] answer, reply; [2] respond, react,
[3] order; [4] send

ANSWER may be done with one or both hands. It means "order" only in the sense of ordering dinner, ordering the car to be brought around, ordering clothes from the catalog, etc.

COMMAND and ANSWER are often used interchangeably.

It may be beneficial to pause here and review the differences between TELL, ANSWER, and COMMAND.

TELL: note the direction the palm faces, inward, toward the body.

ANSWER: the palm is outward, away from the body.

COMMAND: a combination of TELL and ANSWER; it begins like TELL, then changes to ANSWER.
The clauses, "tell me," "answer me," and "command me" look very similar to each other. "Tell me" and "command me" begin in the same way. "Tell me" tends to move from the lips directly to the chest, while "command me" moves from the lips outward before indexing "me." "Answer me" is often done exactly like "command me."

There are other ways to sign SEND, the most common of which is:

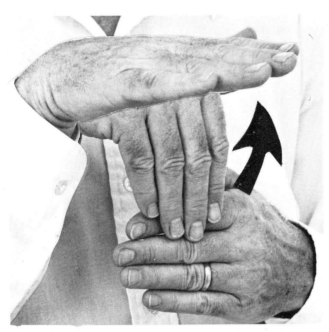

SEND
to send

Sign: (BSF) TURTLE ANSWER-RU//
(BSR) YES//.

Your body actually shifts as you sign ANSWER-RU.

ANSWER must move upwards to reinforce the picture of the height difference between the two.

6. " 'Very well. Are you ready?' asked the hare."

Sign: (BSL) FINE!
　　　　ALLRIGHT!//READY?//

The BSL eliminates the need to sign, "asked the hare," for it is obvious who is talking, also FINE! or ALLRIGHT! may be signed while body shifting.

7. " 'Ready,' replied the tortoise."

Sign: (BSR) READY//

8. " 'Fox, will you be the starter?' the hare asked."

FOX
fox

SHOOT-PISTOL
to shoot a pistol

The idea here is that the "starter" shoots a pistol into the air to start the race.

110

When S uses BSL here, he must address the fox in a place slightly different from where the tortoise has been, and certainly not D, but on the same level for the fox and hare would be equal in height.

Sign: (BSF) RABBIT QUERY-L FOX// (BSL) YOU? PISTOL-SHOOT-U? PLEASE? YOU?//

9. "The fox stepped up and said, 'On your marks, set, go!' "

A gesture that tells a person where to go, move to, or sit

Sign: (BSF) FOX LH: FINGER-PERSON-L—S SPEAK//(BSR) "finger gesture: move, once for the hare, again for the tortoise, to go to the starting line" READY//PISTOL SHOOT-U//.

10. "The hare took off in a cloud of dust, while the tortoise lumbered slowly behind."

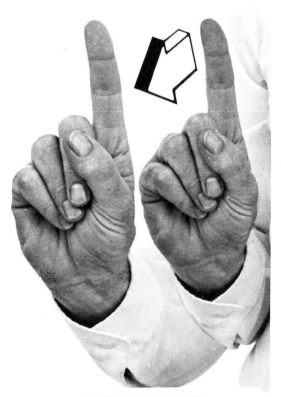

FINGER-PERSON
represents a person, animal, or object that moves

This sign is useful in showing relationships between things. The palm represents the front of the thing. Naturally it is multidirectional. The MEET sign is actually two FINGER-PERSON signs coming together.

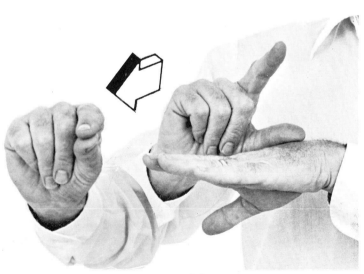

ZOOM
depart quickly, take off in a hurry, run away

(Review MEET, page 63)

CLOUD
[1] cloud; [2] smoke; [3] dust; [4] fog

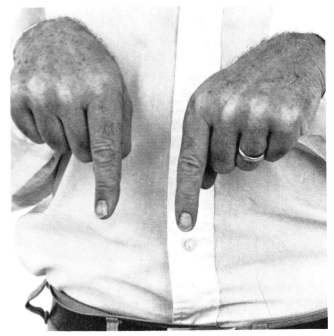

FINGER-LEGS
fingers represent legs, and are moved
according to the type action the legs
moved

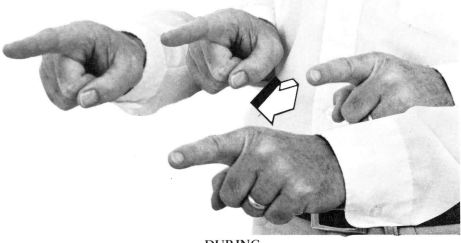

DURING
[1] during, while; [2] parallel

DURING is used in expressions that talk
about two events happening simultaneously. In the sentence, for example: "When I
was a boy, we had no TV," the two simul-
taneous events are: (1) I was a boy, and
(2) there was no TV. So, you sign it:
LONG-AGO DURING ME BOY CHILD//
HAVE T–V NONE//.

Try using FINGER-LEGS to show: tiptoe-
ing, trudging through deep snow, stepping
in water, then shaking the leg to get rid of
the water, extracting a foot from deep
mud.

112

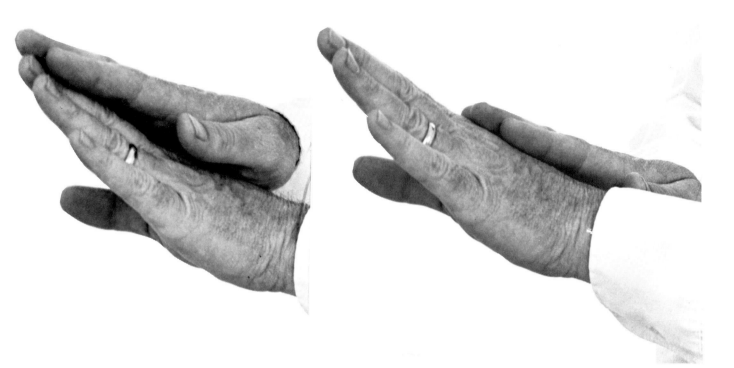

SLOW
slow, slowly

BEHIND
behind, to get behind something physically

FOLLOW
to follow

113

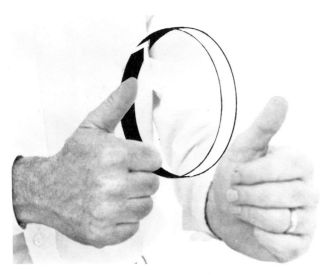

CHASE
to chase, pursue

AVOID
[1] to avoid, be evasive; [2] to fall
behind physically, or figuratively as in,
"...fall behind in loan payments..."

CATCH-UP
to catch up, both physically and figuratively

114

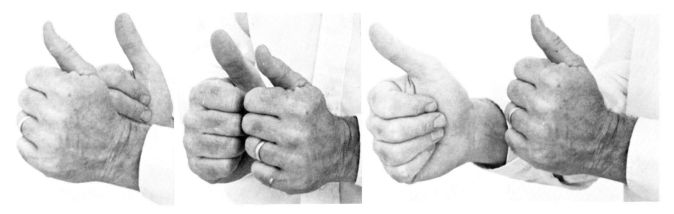

PASS
to pass physically and figuratively as
in "pass a test"

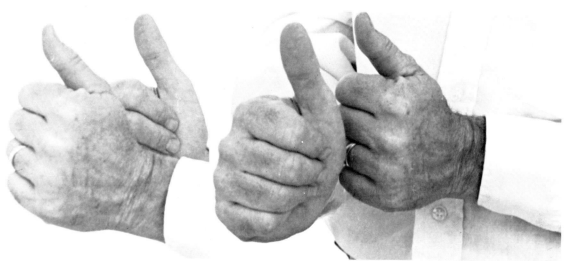

GET-IN-FRONT-OF
to get in front of, to get ahead of,
to pass physically

Sign: (BSF) RABBIT ZOOM-R CLOUD//
TURTLE IT-RD FINGER-LEGS (move
slowly in circles as a turtle's legs do) SLOW
AVOID (separate hands, letting LH slowly
fall behind RH).

11. "After awhile, the hare stopped, and sat down
to rest, knowing the tortoise to be hopelessly
behind."

This sentence is out of sequence, so first re-
write it:

1   After awhile the hare stops,

2. he knows the tortoise is hopelessly behind,

3. so he sits down to rest.

STOP
[1] stop, cease; [2] pause

FAR
far, distant, distance

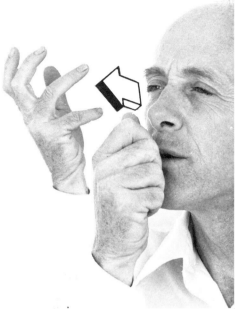

WARM
warm physically and figuratively as
"a warm person"

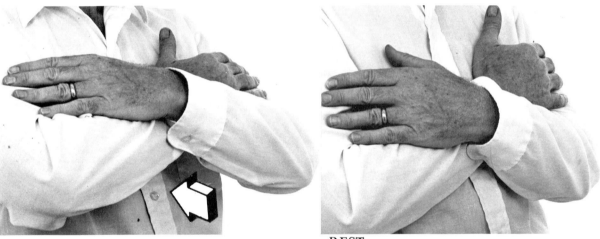

REST
rest, relax, recuperate

There is no sign for, "hopelessly," so to convey this idea sign: CATCH-UP CAN'T//.

Sign: LATER (slowly) RABBIT STOP// KNOW TURTLE INDEX (over shoulder) FAR (turn and do towards area behind S) CATCH-UP CAN'T// "so shrug" DECIDE SIT REST//.

When LATER is done slowly, it indicates a certain amount of time has passed, "a while later." DECIDE is often put in as it is here.

12. "The warm sun made the hare drowsy, and he fell into a deep sleep."

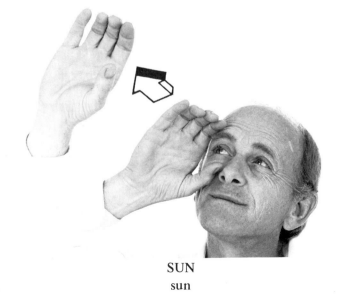

SUN
sun

SLEEP
sleep, asleep, sleeping, sleepy

To indicate "drowsy," repeat SLEEP with languid, brushing movements of the fingers.

ROCK
rock, stone

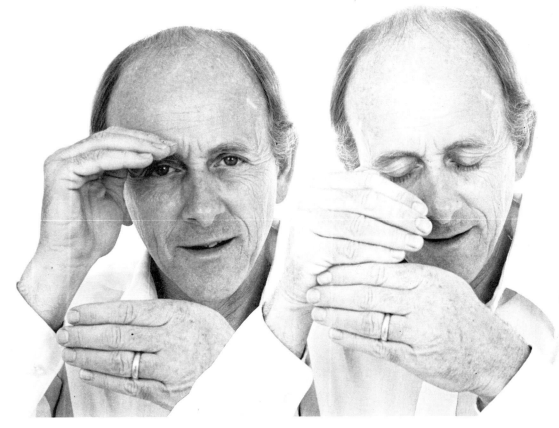

CLOSE-EYES
closing of the eyelids, fall asleep

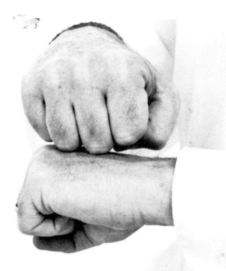

SOLID
[1] hard, solid; [2] rock, stone

Sometimes ROCK and SOLID are done together, and it usually means "rock."

Sign: //SUN LIGHT-RAYS-UR-DL WARM//RABBIT BECOME SLEEP (drowsy) CLOSE-EYES SOLID//.

There is a sign for "make," but here BECOME is better. Ameslan prefers to say, "the hare became drowsy," rather than, "made the hare drowsy." Be sure your facial expression shows "drowsiness."

13. "By and by, the tortoise shuffled up."

Sign: LATER (slowly) TURTLE FINGER-PERSON (on R, as if coming from behind S to the front of S) TURTLE (move it, wobbling as a turtle does)//.

The wobbling motion S gives the TURTLE sign shows his "shuffling."

14. "He gave the sleeping hare a glance, and trudged on toward the finish line."

TO, or UNTIL
[1] to, toward; [2] until

When "to" is meant, RH moves directly to LH. When "until" is meant, RH moves to LH in an arcing movement.

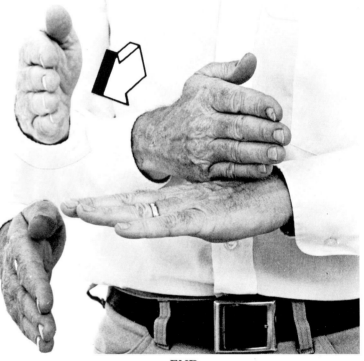

END
[1] the end of something, finis;
[2] finished, completed, over with

Sign: (Make TURTLE stop moving, slowly turn your head toward L.)

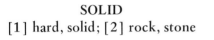

118

LOOK-L//RABBIT SLEEP//(return head front)//TURTLE (move, wobbling off to R) CONTINUE-R TO-R END-R IT-R//.

The IT-R refers to the finish line, not to the turtle.

15. "About a half-hour later, a fly lit on the hare's nose and awakened him."

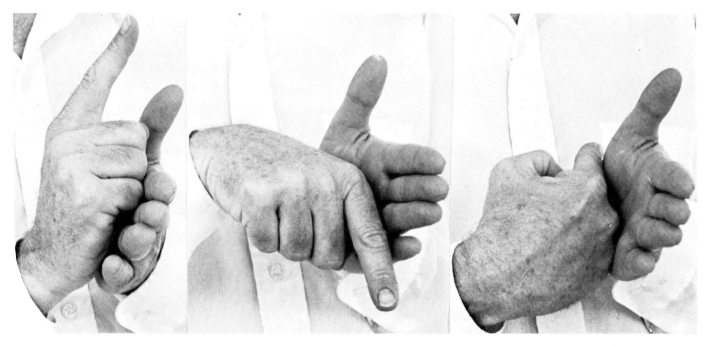

HOUR
hour

HOUR
hour

MINUTE
minute, moment

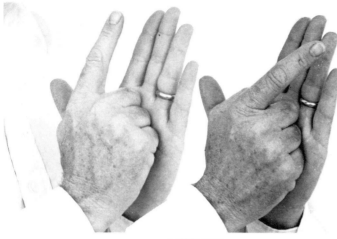

MINUTE
minute, moment

L

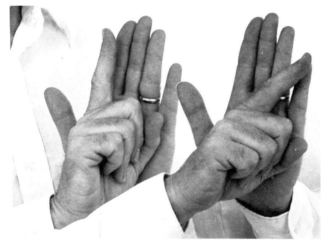

MINUTE
minute, moment

If you make **MINUTE** the third way, then you can continue twisting the hand downward to get:

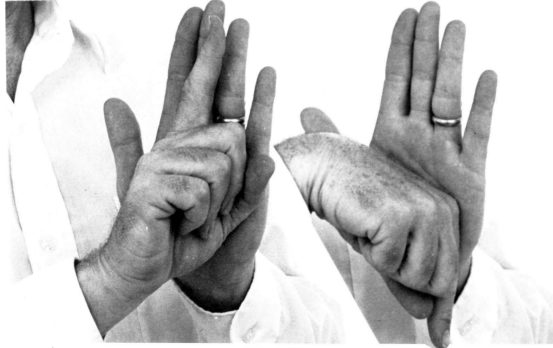

HALF-HOUR
a half an hour

Using the HALF-HOUR sign is sufficient to convey the idea, "About a half-hour later."

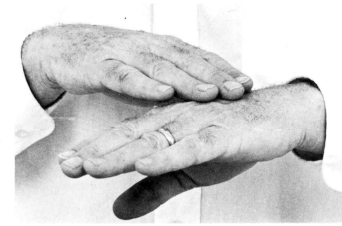

ON
on, on top of

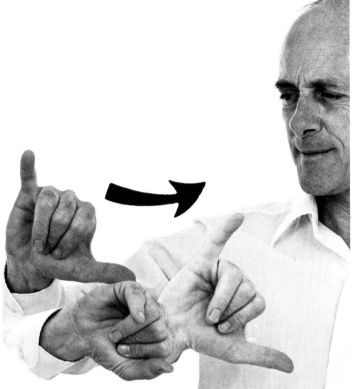

FLYING-INSECT
any flying creature, but usually
an insect

There is no sign for "fly," though the INSECT sign could be used. I prefer here to fingerspell, F—L—Y, then show the insect flying.

Most parts of the anatomy have no signs. One merely indexes them or touches them.

Sign: HALF-HOUR HAPPEN F—L—Y FLYING-INSECT (let it buzz around) ON RABBIT ITS-L "index nose" FLYING-INSECT (land the "fly" on S's nose)// AWAKE!//.

INSECT
any insect or bug

AWAKE, or SURPRISE
[1] awake, wake up; [2] surprise

16. "The hare leaped to his feet, and dashed for the finish line."

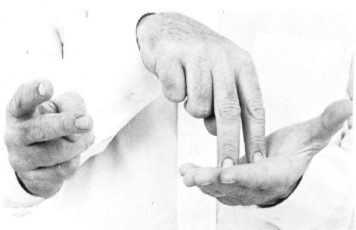

STAND-UP
to stand up from a sitting or prone position

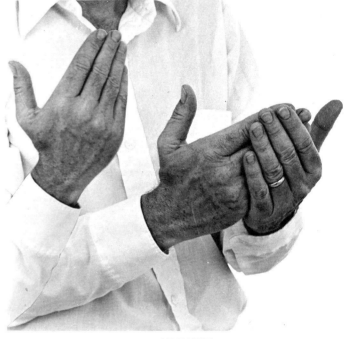

ARRIVE
arrive, reach a place, get there

Sign: STAND-UP!//RAPID-RUN-R ZOOM-R//.

There is no need to sign, "for the finish line." Since W knows the finish line was established R of S by the tortoise moving in that direction, and the signing of END in sentence 14, and since the RAPID-RUN sign moves R, the hare is obviously running toward it.

Sign: RABBIT ARRIVE-R//SEE-R TURTLE IT-R SIT//(BSL) SMILE//.

17. "Just as the hare reached the finish line, he saw the tortoise sitting on the other side, smiling."

122

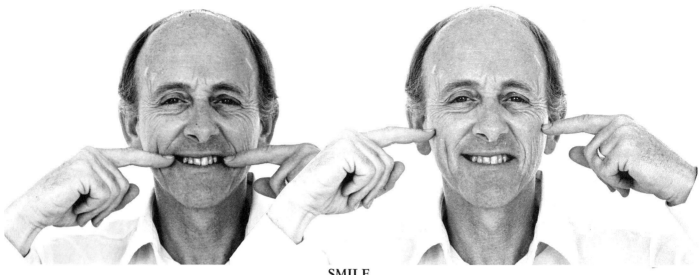

SMILE
smile

18. " 'You tricked me!' screamed the hare, 'I'm faster than you are, and you know it!' "

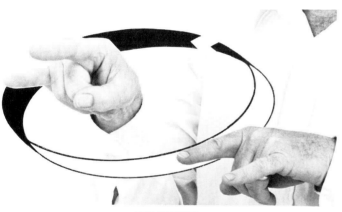

DECEIVE
deceive, trick

FAST
fast, quick

FAST is not quite as fast as RAPID.

YELL
yell, shout, scream

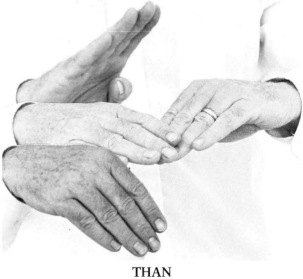

THAN
than

123

KNOW-WELL
emphatic know, know very well,
be well acquainted with

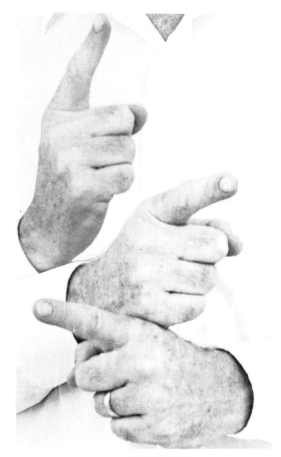

CORRECT
[1] correct, right, proper; [2] when
repeated, means "regularly;" [3] idiomatically: "that's normal," "it's to be
expected"

Sign: (BSF) RABBIT YELL//(BSR) YOU
DECEIVE-W—S ME!// FAST! COMP.!
THAN! YOU!//KNOW-WELL! YOU!//.

Notice that now S must BSR to play the
role of the hare. This happens because of
the changed positions of the hare and tortoise, which was spatialized by the AR-
RIVE-R and SEE-R in sentence 17.

Also notice that RABBIT YELL precedes
the thing he yells.

19. " 'Mebbe so,' drawled the tortoise, 'but speed
up 'n' stop won't never beat slow 'n' steady.' "

NEVER
never

124

WIN
win, victory

ALWAYS
always

ALWAYS and ONLY are often indistinguishable.

Sign: (BSF) TURTLE SPEAK//(BSL) MAYBE CORRECT//DON'T-KNOW//BUT RAPÍD-L STOP-L//RAPID-L STOP-L// BEAT-R SLOW-R CONTINUE-R// NEVER//IT-R WIN ALWAYS//.

The idea of "steady" is conveyed by making the CONTINUE sign in small circles.

Ameslan expands on the moral by adding, that slow and steady always wins. The spatialization R and L of the two ways (speed up 'n' stop vs. slow 'n' steady) creates a clearer picture of the two things being compared.

COMPLETE TRANSLATION

Practice it, try to memorize it!

ONCE LONG-AGO //RABBIT IT-R BRAG// ME RAPID-RUN ME//CHALLENGE ANIMAL "gesture to the 'animals' "// COMPETE? WANT;//.

HAPPEN TURTLE IT-LD ACCEPT CHALLENGE ACCEPT//.

(BSL) YOU!//THINK BEAT W—S? CAN? YOU?//

(BSF) TURTLE ANSWER-RU//.

(BSR) YES//.

(BSL) FINE!
     ALLRIGHT! READY?//.

(BSR) READY//.

(BSF) RABBIT QUERY-L//FOX//.

(BSL) YOU? PISTOL - SHOOT - U? PLEASE? YOU?//.

(BSF) FOX LH:FINGER-PERSON-L—S SPEAK//

(BSR) "finger gesture: move; once for hare, again for the tortoise to go to the starting line"//READY //PISTOL-SHOOT U//.

(BSF) RABBIT ZOOM-R CLOUD//TURTLE IT-RD FINGER-LEGS (move slowly in circles as a turtle's legs do) SLOW AVOID (separate hands, letting LH slowly fall behind RH)//.

LATER (slowly) RABBIT STOP KNOW TURTLE INDEX (over shoulder) FAR (turn toward area toward S) CATCH-UP CAN'T//"so" DECIDE SIT REST// SUN RAYS-UR-DL WARM//RABBIT BECOME SLEEP (drowsy) CLOSE-EYES SOLID//.

LATER (slowly)//TURTLE FINGER - PERSON (on R, as if coming from behind S to the front of S) TURTLE (move it, wobbling as a turtle does)// (make TURTLE stop moving, slowly turn your head toward L) LOOK-L//RABBIT SLEEP//(return head front)//TURTLE (wobbling off to R) CONTINUE-R TO-R END-R IT-R//.

HALF-HOUR HAPPEN FLY FLYING - INSECT (let it buzz around) ON RABBIT ITS-L "index nose" FLYING-INSECT (land the "fly" on S's nose)//AWAKE!//STAND - UP!//RAPID - RUN-R ZOOM-R//RABBIT ARRIVE-R//SEE-R TURTLE IT-R SIT//.

(BSL) SMILE//.
(BSF) RABBIT YELL
(BSR) YOU DECEIVE-W-S// ME! FAST COMP.! THAN! YOU!// KNOW-WELL! YOU!//.
(BSF) TURTLE SPEAK//.

(BSL)MAYBE CORRECT//DON'T - KNOW//BUT RAPID-L STOP-L//RAPID-L STOP-L//BEAT-R SLOW-R CONTINUED-R NEVER//IT-R WIN AL-WAYS//.

NEW SIGNS TO REVIEW

ABOUT	HALF-HOUR
ACCEPT	HAPPEN
ALWAYS	HOUR
ANIMAL	HUMBLE
ANSWER	INSECT
ARRIVE	KNOW-WELL
AVOID	MINUTE
AWAKE	NEVER
BEAT	ON
BEHIND	OTHER
BRAG	PASS
CAN	RABBIT
CATCH-UP	RAPID
CHALLENGE	RAPID-RUN
CHASE	REST
CLOSE-EYES	ROCK
CLOUD	RUN
COMMAND	SEND
COMPETE	SHOOT-PISTOL
CORRECT	SLEEP
DECEIVE	SLOW
DURING	SMILE
END	SOLID
FAR	STAND-UP
FAST	STOP
FINGER-LEGS	SUN
FINGER-PERSON	THAN
FLYING-INSECT	TO
FOLLOW	TURTLE
FOX	WARM
GET-IN-FRONT-OF	WIN
	YELL
	ZOOM

"Go there! Move there! Sit there!"

F—I—N—G—E—R—S—P—E—L—L—I—N—G

"L"

NOTES

LESSON 14

A rhetorical question is a question which the speaker asks, but does not expect anyone to answer, such as, "My! Don't you look lovely today?"

It is usually asked to create an effect. Ameslan uses the rhetorical question in the same way, but much more frequently than English does. S may sign, MAN-R IT-R SPEAK WHAT-SHRUG//NO-R-S!//, which would mean, "What did he say to me? I'll tell you what he said, he said 'No!'"

ADDITIONAL VOCABULARY

WHY
why? what for?

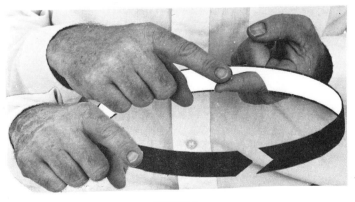

WHEN
when?

PROCEED
[1] proceed, go ahead, move on;
[2] get along with a person

When the **THINK SELF** signs are done together it means, "Do as you wish," "Make up your own mind," etc.

EXERCISE 20

Translate each of these sentences, incorporating in each one a rhetorical question.

1. He gave her the book last night.

2. I'm going to a movie tomorrow afternoon.

3. I don't know which to accept.

4. He's the one who told me.

5. I knew because she told me.

6. I'll leave when you've given me the book.

7. I went home because he told me to.

8. That's what I want to know.

9. If you want to learn, then you must ask me questions.

10. If that's what you want, go ahead.

NEW SIGNS TO REVIEW

PROCEED   WHEN   WHY

130

NOTES

LESSON

In Exercise 15 on page 37, you re-arranged the sentences in order to get them into the proper time-sequence. Now you will learn to sign these sentences and paragraphs.

1. We had lots of fun then, even though we had no automobiles to take us anywhere.

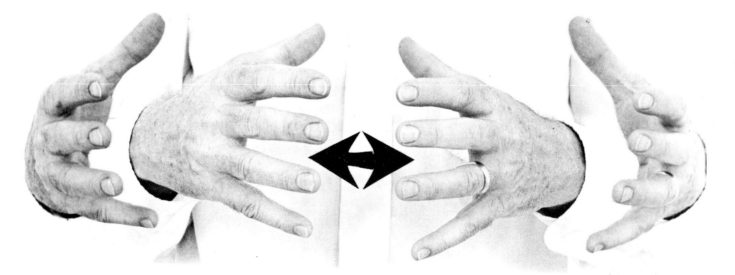

MUCH
much, a large amount, a lot of,
abundant

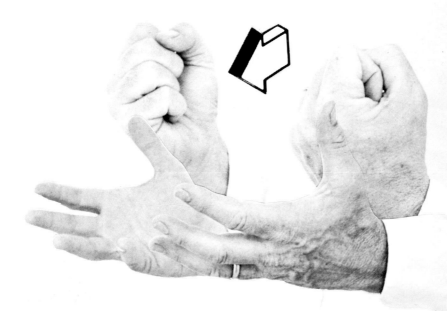

MANY
many, numerous, a large number of,
a lot of

CAR
[1] car, automobile; [2] drive a car

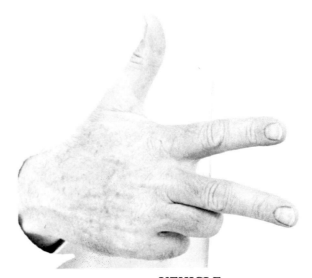

VEHICLE
almost any type vehicle or boat
(particularly useful spatializating the object)

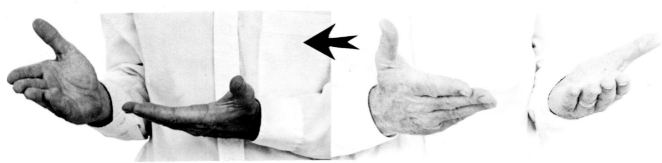

BRING
bring, take, carry, convey, transport

134

TOUR
[1] tour, touring, traveling; [2] running
around all over the place

FUN
[1] fun, good time; [2] humor,
humorous; [3] joke

Sign: LONG - AGO (WE) HAVE CAR
TOUR
CARRY-L-R NONE//BUT NO-MATTER//
TER//

HAVE FUN
BH:PLEASE MUCH TRUE//

2. I like nothing so much as a tall, cool glass
of iced tea when I come in all sweaty from
mowing the lawn on a hot summer day.

FUNNY
funny, humorous, comic

SUMMER
summer, summertime

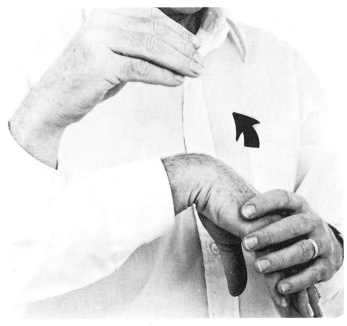

OUT
out, outside

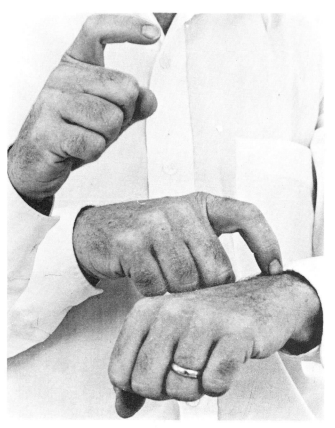

TIME
[1] time, time of day; [2] times, as in.
"I've seen it three times"

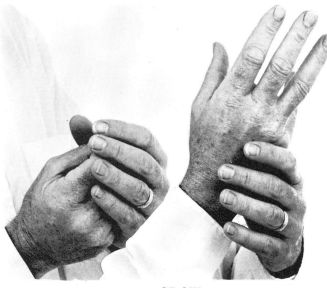

GROW
[1] grow, develop; [2] spring, springtime (often followed by the TIME-ERA
sign)

TIME-ERA
[1] era, epoch; [2] a period of time

("Springtime," "In my time...," "He stayed
a long time," etc.)

PUSH-CART
a push cart, grocery cart, lawn mower
baby carriage, etc.

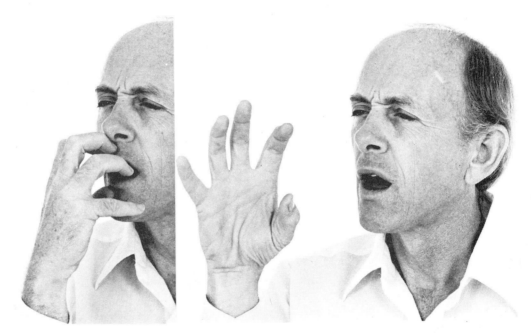

HOT
hot physically and figuratively

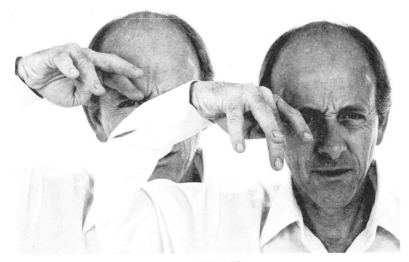

SWEAT
sweat, sweaty, perspiration

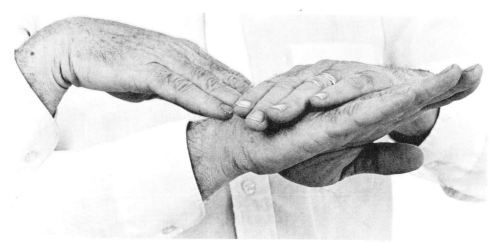

ENTER
[1] enter, go into; [2] into

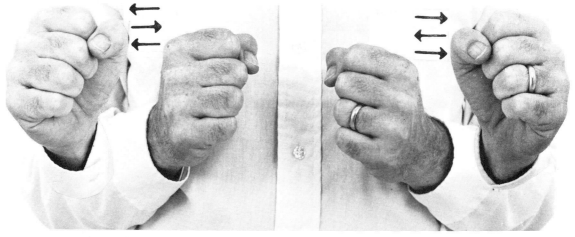

COLD
[1] cold, cool physically and figuratively; [2] winter (often followed by TIME-
ERA

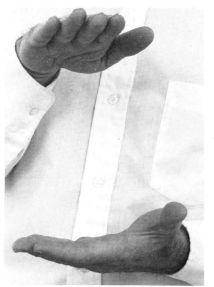

HEIGHT
an indication of vertical length or height,
or of vertical size (when the height is too
tall for both hands, use only the upper
hand)

GLASS, or CUP
a container of any sort

GET
get, receive, acquire, obtain

CITY
city, town, village, community

HOUSE
house

There is no standard sign for "grass," so fingerspell it.

G

Sign: DURING SUMMER//ME OUT-R G–R–A–S–S PUSH-CART (several directions)// HOT//SWEAT//FINISH//ENTER-L HOUSE-L// GET GLASS HEIGHT (tall glass) TEA//COLD//DRINK PLEASE GOOD MOST//.

If you wished to use the rehetorical question, you could sign the sentence:

DURING SUMMER//ME OUT-R G–R–A–S–S PUSH-CART (several directions)// HOT // SWEAT FINISH//ENTER-L HOUSE-L// WANT DRINK MOST WHAT-SHRUG// GLASS HEIGHT (tall glass) TEA COLD DRINK//PLEASE//.

3. I hate to get out of bed on cold, rainy mornings, but once I'm up, I'm okay.

4. Isn't it odd how we seem unable to run fast in our dreams, but rather keep falling down, or else run in slow motion as if our shoes were made of lead.

BORED
[1] bore, boring, boredom;
[2] hate, intense dislike

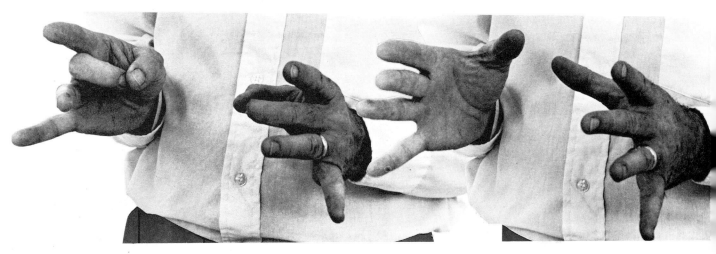

HATE
hate, dislike intensely, abhor, malice

Sign: DURING MORNING//COLD//RAIN//STAND-UP BORED // BUT STAND-UP FINISH//FEEL FINE
HATE   ALL RIGHT

140

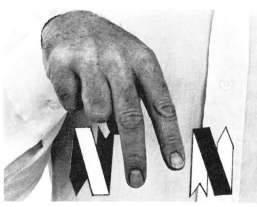

FINGER-WALK
depicts a person walking or running

IN
in inside

DREAM
dream

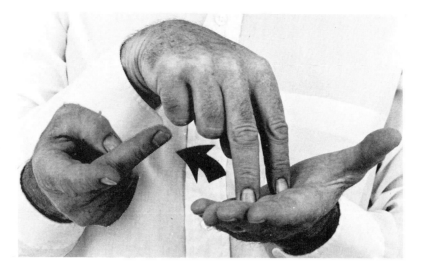

FALL
a fall, fall down

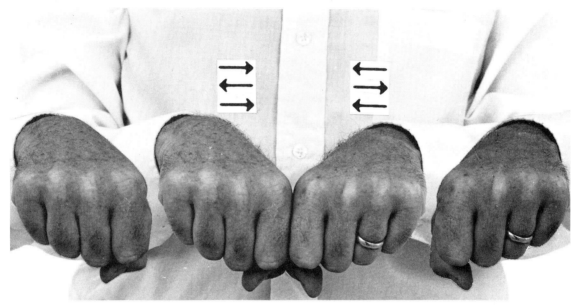

SHOE
shoe, shoes

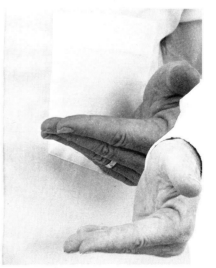

HEAVY
heavy, physically and figuratively

142

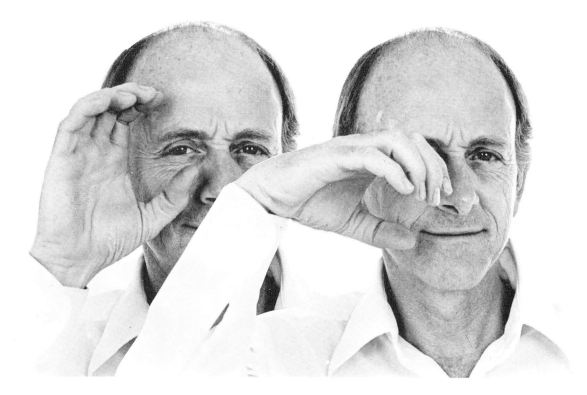

ODD
odd, strange, queer, peculiar

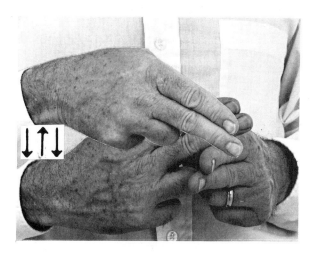

WEIGH
[1] weigh, weight; [2] pounds

5. I finally got to England last summer, something I had always wanted to do.

Sign: DURING DREAM//RAPID‑RUN TRY CAN'T//FINGER‑LEGS (slow motion) FINGER‑WALK (slow motion running) FALL-R// STAND‑UP// FINGER‑WALK (slow motion running) FALL-L// STAND-UP// SEEM SHOE WEIGH HEAVY SEEM// ODD TRUE//.

LIVE
[1] live, alive; [2] life; [3] address
(often initialized with "L's," especially
for "live" and "life")

6. If ever you get to London, be sure to visit
Westminster Cathedral. I saw it a few years
ago and was immensely impressed with it.
There are many famous people buried
there, and I felt as if I had met them just
by seeing their graves.

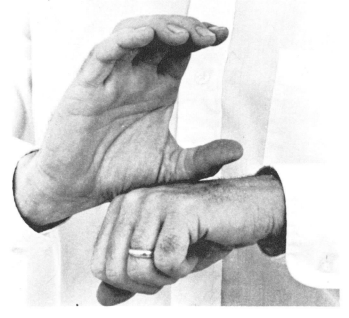

CHURCH
church, cathedral

ENGLAND
[1] England; [2] English

SUCCESS
[1] success, succeed; [2] achievement,
attainment; [3] idiomatically, "At
last!" "It's finally done!"

TEMPLE
temple, synagogue

FAMOUS
[1] famous, noted, eminent, well known; [2] idiomatically: someone is well known for some particular trait or quirk

PEOPLE
[1] people; [2] humanity, society

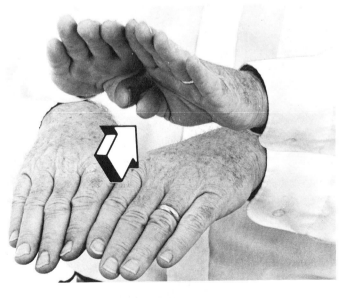

GRAVE
[1] grave, tomb; [2] graveyard, cemetery; [3] bury, funeral

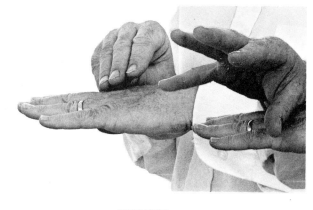

IMPRESS
[1] impressive, affect deeply;
[2] emphasize, stress, accentuate

ADVISE
[1] advise, advice, counsel;
[2] influence, affect

W

Sign: SEVERAL YEAR PAST//ME GO-TO-R//VISIT-R L-O-N-D-O-N//DURING INDEX-R//ME GO TO-L VISIT-L W-E-S-T-M-I-N-S-T-E-R CHURCH// MANY FAMOUS PEOPLE GRAVE IT-L //ME LOOK-LD (move it in LD area)// FEEL MEET-LD3 FINISH//IMPRESS-L-S//WOW!//YOU GO-TO-R LONDON// ADVISE VISIT-L CHURCH-L INDEX-L //ADVISE//.

7. "Oh! I'm terribly sorry!" he said, then he picked up the packages strewn all over the floor, which was the result of him bumping into me.

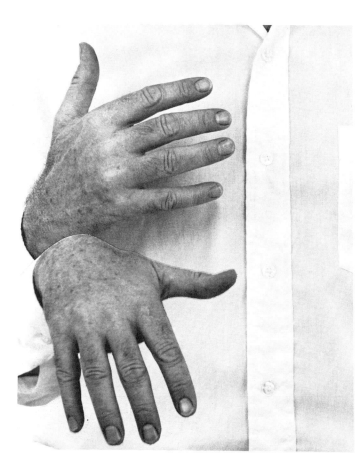

WOW
wow! my goodness!

SORRY
sorry, regret, be sorry

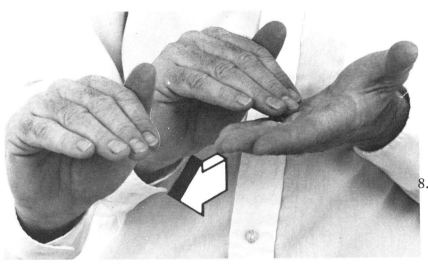

EXCUSE
[1] excuse me, forgive me, pardon me;
[2] excuse, pardon

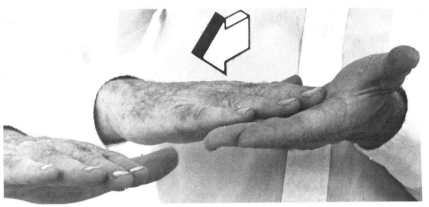

PARDON
[1] you're pardoned, you're excused,
you're forgiven; [2] to lay off or be laid
off from a job

Sign: ME BOX-3 (several small ones) L–R "mime carrying them"//HAPPEN MAN-R RH: FINGER- PERSON LH: FINGER PERSON "RH approaches LH, and 'bumps' into it" BOX "gesture indicating the boxes falling from your hands"// MAN SPEAK (BSL) SORRY//EXCUSE//ME "mime picking up the boxes, then handing them L, i.e., to S."

8. Ivan the Terrible ordered St. Basil's Cathedral to be built during the 16th century in honor of Russia's liberation from the Tartars, which occurred in the 15th century. Mocking the austerity of the martial parades, and the spartan simplicity of Lenin's tomb, St. Basil's sits on Red Square looking as if it had been sculptured in chocolate, vanilla, and pistachio ice cream. (With apologies to Jack Smith of the LOS ANGELES TIMES.)

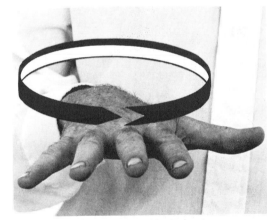

AREA
[1] an area, a space, piece of ground;
[2] field, meadow, pasture; [3] land,
nation, country; [4] approximation
when used with number

RUSSIA
Russia, Russian

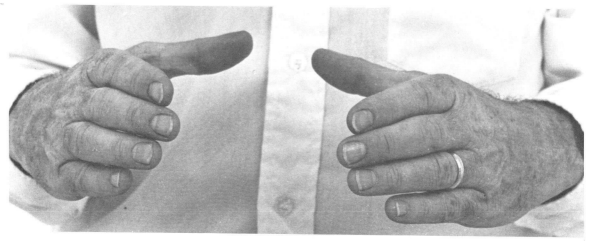

GROUP
a group of people or things, used mainly
for spatializing

CLASS
a class or group

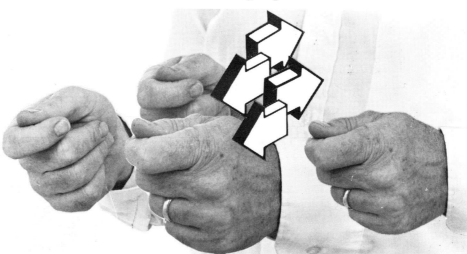

CONTROL
[1] control, manage, direct; [2] rule
over, reign; [3] steer or drive horses

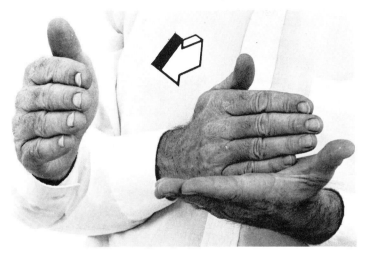

BANISH
banish, ban, reject, cast out

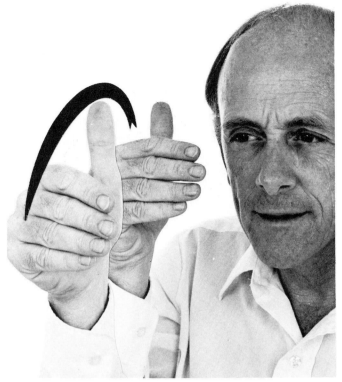

NEXT-FUTURE
later on, sometime in the future

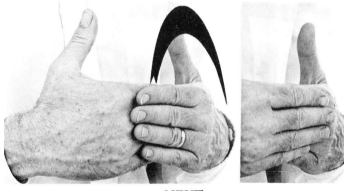
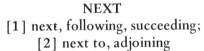

NEXT
[1] next, following, succeeding;
[2] next to, adjoining

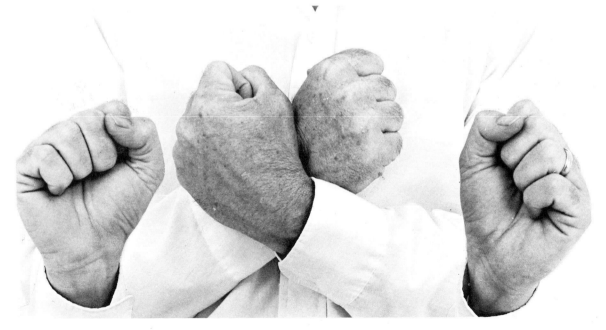

FREE
[1] free, freedom, liberty; [2] saved, salvation (often initialized, "F" for "freedom," "L" for liberty; when
"F" "freedom" is done small, it usually means "free, no charge")

ESTABLISH
establish, found, set up, erect

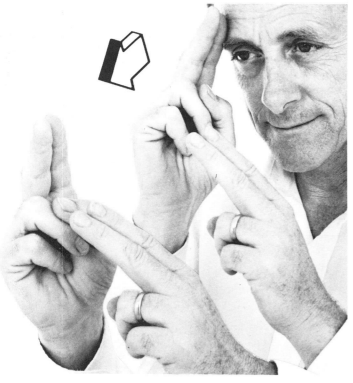

HONOR
honor, respect (sometimes "respect"
is initialized with "R's")

FACE
[1] face; [2] look, as in, "He looks like
his father")

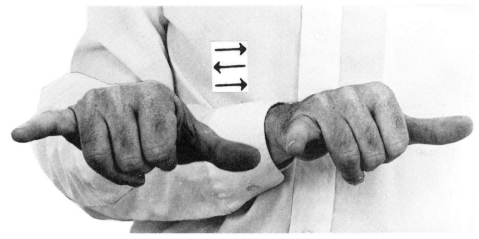

SAME
same, similar, alike, identical

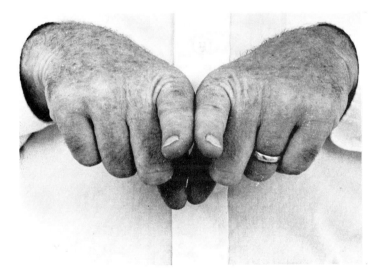

AS
as, like, alike, same identical

SAME and AS are usually interchangeable. SAME tends to be used more with concrete ideas, and AS with abstract ones, but this usage is at the discretion of S.

ICE-CREAM
ice cream, ice cream cone

151

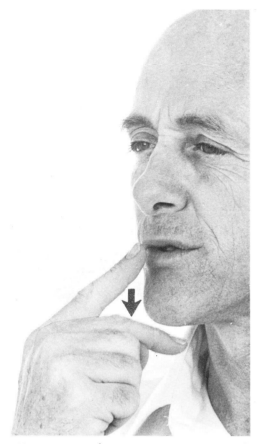

"A turret with an ice cream type swirl on top"

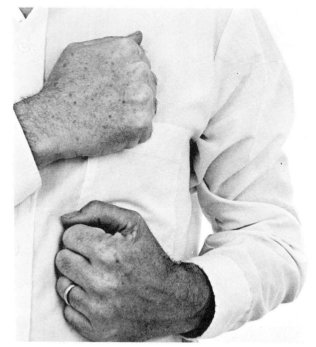

ARMY
army, military, soldier

Q

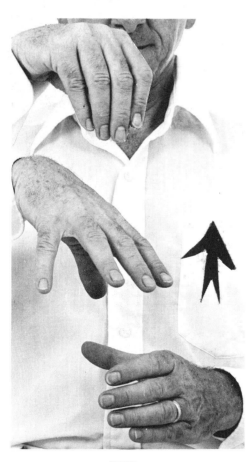

RED
red

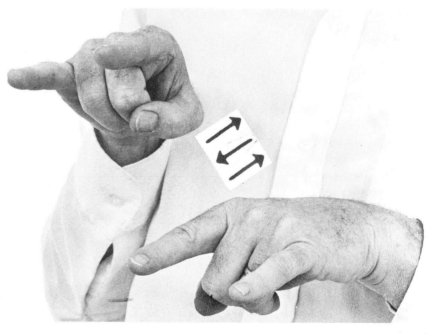

LAUGH-AT
laugh at, make fun of, mock

LAUGH
laugh

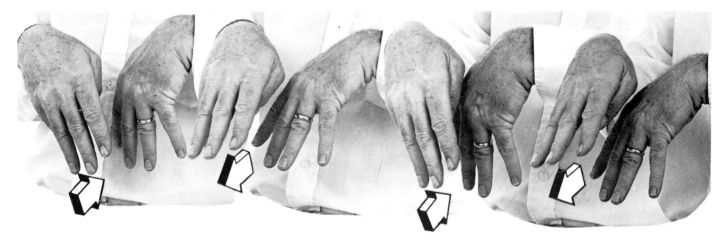

PARADE
parade, march

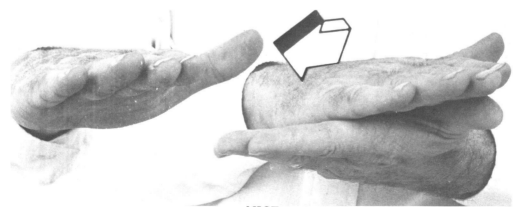

NICE
[1] nice, clean, neat; [2] simple,
plain, unadorned

153

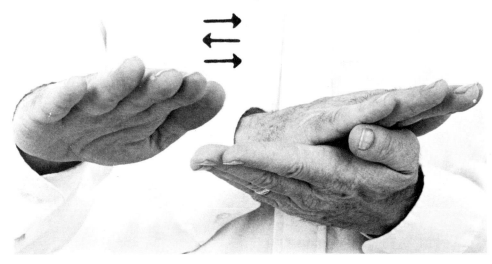

CLEAN
clean up, tidy up, make neat

The only difference between the action of NICE and CLEAN is that NICE has one movement, while CLEAN has two. CLEAN could be written NICE[2].

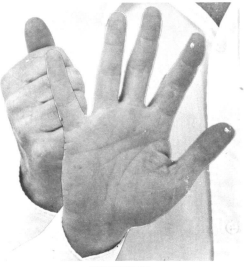

FIFTEEN

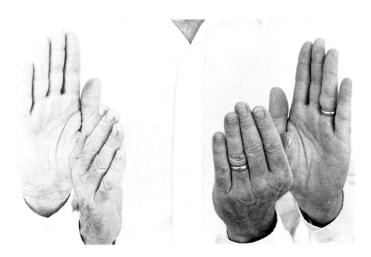

COMPARE
compare, comparison

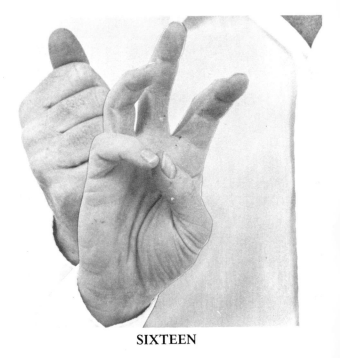

SIXTEEN

154

ELABORATE
dressy, showy, elaborate, ornate

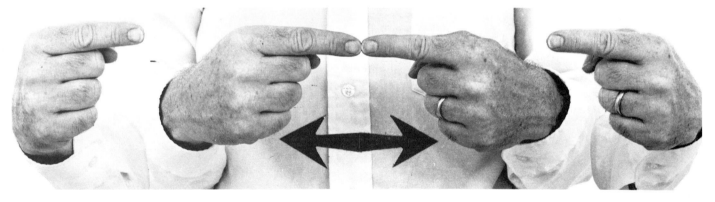

OPPOSITE
[1] opposite; [2] disagree (sometimes
THINK comes just before OPPOSITE)

Sign:

LONG-AGO RUSSIA INDEX-R // PEOPLE-L GROUP-L NAME-L T–A–R–T–A–R–S // INDEX-L CONTROL AREA-R-L RUSSIA // BUT DURING 15–T–H C–E–N–T–U–R–Y // RUSSIA SUCCESS BEAT-L // BANISH-L // FREE // SUCCESS! // NEXT-FUTURE DURING 16–T–H C–E–N–T–U–R–Y RUSSIA CONTROL AGENT MAN NAME I–V–A–N T–H–E T–E–R–R–I–B–L–E // INDEX-R COMMAND ESTABLISH CHURCH HONOR-L LONG-AGO FREE // CHURCH ESTABLISH NAME S–T B–A–S–I–L // CHURCH FACE [SAME/AS] ICE-CREAM "indicate 2 or 3 turrets with the swirl on top" // NOW CHURCH ESTABLISH ON RED S–Q–U–A–R–E // DURING`ARMY PARADE-L-R // SEEM CHURCH INDEX-R-U LAUGH-AT-LD-RD//L–E–N–I–N GRAVE INDEX-LD NICE-L ELABORATE NOT//COMPARE-LD-RU CHURCH// ELABORATE-RU//OPPOSITE-LD-RU//SEEM INDEX-RU LAUGH-AT-LD//SEEM//

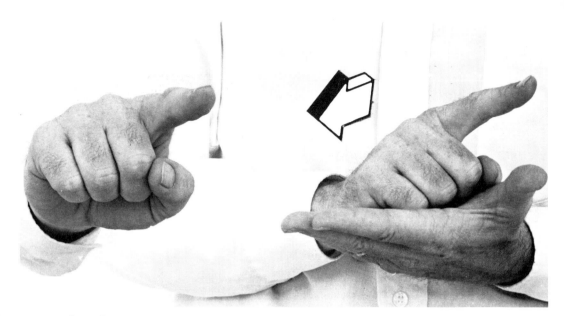

WEEK
week

9. We were all greatly concerned at the news that Walter had been struck on the head by a falling tree last week. He had been out tramping through the woods at the time, and had taken shelter under a tree, when a thunderstorm blew up. Lightning struck the tree, and Walter was hit by one of the lower branches of the tree as it fell.

TREE
tree

WEEK-AGO
a week ago, last week, the past week

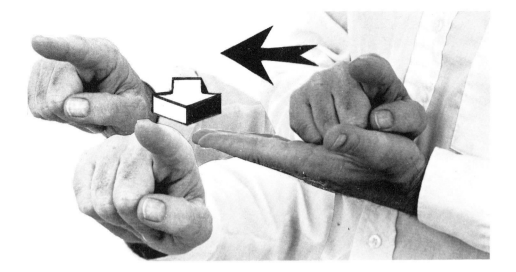

NEXT–WEEK
next week, a week from now

WALK
walk, take a walk, go for a walk, stroll

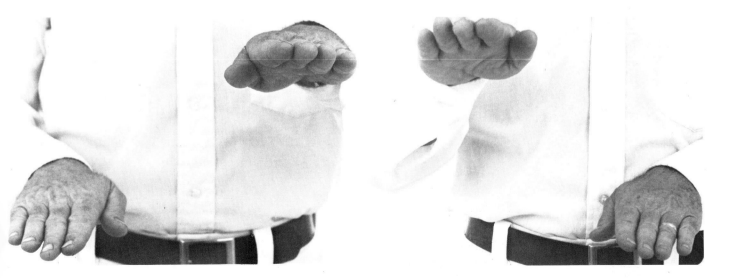

WALK
walk, take a walk, go for a walk, stroll

WALK
walk, take a **walk**, go for a walk, stroll

WALK
walk, take a walk, go for a walk, stroll

STAND
stand, standing

WRONG
[1] wrong, mistake, error;
[2] idiomatically: an accident, something happened that should not have
happened

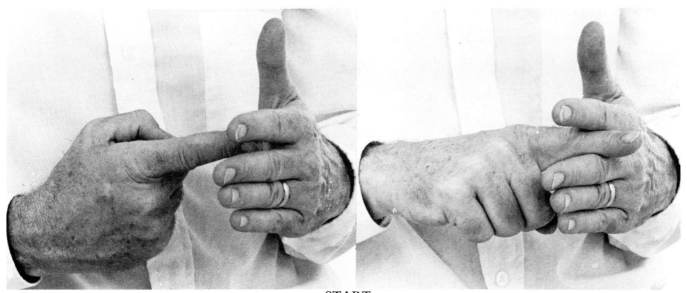

START
start, begin, commence

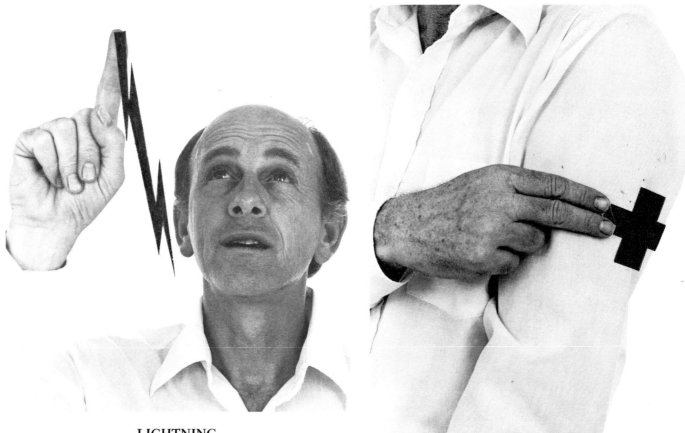

LIGHTNING
lightning, bolt of lightning, thunderbolt

HOSPITAL
hospital, infirmary

WORRY
[1] worry, concern, fret; [2] trouble;
[3] problem

Sign:

WEEK-AGO W–A–L–T–E–R GO-TO-R TREE-R-L // WALK-R FINGER-PERSON-R // HAPPEN BLACK CLOUD // START RAIN // RAPID-RUN-L // LH:TREE RH:STAND (next to tree) // WRONG // LIGHTNING-RU (zig-zag DL and hit tree) // "make the tree start to fall, then stop and with RH index little finger of LH, to establish 'a limb' " // "strike your head with edge of LH" // "go back to TREE 'falling' with RH-STAND, let the 'limb' hit RH, then RH falls on the ground" // BRING-R HOSPITAL // WE HEAR HAPPEN // WORRY //

NEW SIGNS TO REVIEW

ADVISE	ELABORATE	GROW	NEXT	SORRY	WOW!
AREA	ENGLAND	HATE	NEXT-FUTURE	STAND	WRONG
ARMY	ENTER	HEAVY	NEXT-WEEK	START	
AS	ESTABLISH	HEIGHT	NICE	SUCCESS	G
BANISH	EXCUSE	HONOR	ODD	SUMMER	W
BORED	FACE	HOSPITAL	OPPOSITE	SWEAT	Q
BRING	FALL	HOT	OUT	TEMPLE	
CAR	FAMOUS	HOUSE	PARADE	TIME	
CHURCH	FIFTEEN	ICE-CREAM	PARDON	TIME-ERA	
CITY	FINGER-WALK	IMPRESS	PEOPLE	TOUR	
CLASS	FREE	IN	PUSH-CART	TREE	
CLEAN	FUN	LAUGH	RED	VEHICLE	
COLD	FUNNY	LAUGH-AT	RUSSIA	WALK	
COMPARE	GET	LIGHTNING	SAME	WEEK	
CONTROL	GLASS	LIVE	SHOE	WEEK-AGO	
CUP	GRAVE	MANY	SIXTEEN	WEIGH	
DREAM	GROUP	MUCH	SMILE	WORRY	